SOCIALIZE TO MONETIZE

Engaging Your Online Community
Across Multiple Social Media Platforms

GABRIELA TAYLOR

Legal Notice

The publisher and author have strived to be as accurate and complete as possible in the creation of this book. The contents within are accurate and up to date at the time of writing however the publisher accepts that due to the rapidly changing nature of the Internet some information may not be fully up to date at the time of reading.

Whilst all attempts have been made to verify information provided in this publication, the Publisher assumes no responsibility for errors, omissions, or contrary interpretation of the subject matter herein. Any perceived slights of specific people or organizations are unintentional.

All Rights Reserved

Dedication

This book is dedicated to all the small business start-ups out there and all who wish to utilise the web to its full potential. The opportunities are endless when using social media to maximize the power and reach of your business.

Contents

Introduction

Utilizing Social Media networks to launch, grow and maximize any business or online marketing strategy is absolutely essential in this digitally connected and dependent world. The opportunity to reach a wider community and customer base, grow your network and to stay abreast of social media trends is key to driving success. This can also however be a confusing world where new networks and fads are literally springing up daily. It can be tempting to join an overwhelming number of social media sites without any real idea of how to make the most of your online presence. While most of these platforms are valuable to your brand, it is essential that you know how and when to use them effectively for maximum return. Throughout this book I will cover some of the most popular social networks and how to use them to your advantage and grow your business. You will also learn how to build and engage a community across multiple social media platforms and how to become a master in social link building. That's just few of the things you will learn from this book that will conclude with a list of 17 top social networks for entrepreneurs. By registering with these networks you will get free expert advice and resources on various areas regarding your small business.

Engaging Across Multiple Platforms

"Social media isn't about having a conversation with people you know. It's about advertising yourself. It's not social; it's media... Every time you post something on Twitter, Facebook, Tumblr, or Instagram, you're influencing—or trying to influence—how the world views you... Real conversations don't happen in public. You tell people what you think they want to hear. Mostly that means telling them interesting bits that are designed to make them like you." (Source: **Wired Magazine**)

It is easy to argue the fact that Mashable is top dog when it comes to applying social media in all of its forms. Taking a close look at the company itself, its origins, vision and purpose, can help us better understand how Mashable came to be such an innovator at integrating social media and engaging across multiple platforms. It is safe to say that their example of applying online social media as a business is a good model to follow and this is the reason I decided to talk about Mashable in this introductory chapter.

Pete Cashmore founded the site back in 2005, when he was 19, from his home in Aberdeenshire, Scotland using a computer he borrowed from his parents. Pete's primary purpose from the beginning was to illustrate how social networks and other web tools were altering human interactions in a way that was reshaping entire cultures. The results of his passion became what Mashable is today:

3,400,000+ Followers across Multiple Social Platforms

12,000,000+ Unique Monthly Visitors

40,000+ Daily Retweets on Twitter

40,000+ Facebook Shares per week

Mashable self proclaimed mission is "to empower and inspire" its readers through "spreading social media and technology." They are currently the largest independent news source that dedicates its efforts to monitoring digital culture and social media and technology. They publish daily 45 new stories and are considered by Klout to be the "most influential outlet" for online news and by Hewlett-Packard the "most influential Twitter account", based on the number of links retweeted. Their audience interests as shown by Google AdPlanner are listed below:

Audience Interests

Interest
Brand Management
Venture Capital
Android OS
Search Engine Optimization & Marketing
Writing & Editing Services
Project Management Software
Industrial & Product Design
Feed Aggregation & Social Bookmarking
Web Stats & Analytics
Development Tools

Mashable is currently working in conjunction with top publications like CNN, ABC News, Yahoo and Metro in addition to being present on all major online social media platforms. They also have created in February 2012 their own social network called 'Mashable Follow'. This many-layered approach is allowing Mashable to reach many millions of readers every month.

Which Social Networks Is Mashable Using And When?

Making the most of the social web is more complicated than simply posting random status updates to see 'what sticks'. Mashable has put considerable effort into figuring out the best way to leverage their presence on the various social networks. They consider carefully when it is most effective to post to Facebook or LinkedIn or when they may be better off posting to Twitter or Google+. Almost all of Mashable's content is duplicated across each of the social media sites. However, the way they post their content on each platform depends on the specific platform used. Mashable takes into consideration the audience each site reaches and focuses on what that social media platform is best suited to accomplish.

FACEBOOK

Facebook has more than 900 million users with half of them connecting daily to the site and spending on average of 24 minutes per visit. Mashable considers this site as the best site to interact with contacts on a 'personal level'. Mashable updates its 'Timeline' on Facebook a few times per day.

The largest segment of users on Facebook is aged 25 to 54 years old, 50% male and 50% female (see below demographics from Google AdPlanner). On Facebook, Mashable focuses mostly on blog posts, videos, photos and Q&As.

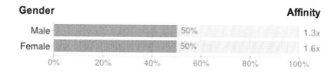

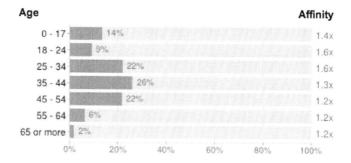

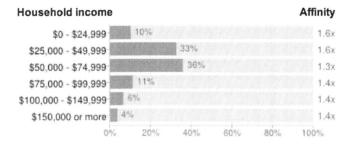

Household income		Affinity
$0 - $24,999	10%	1.6x
$25,000 - $49,999	33%	1.6x
$50,000 - $74,999	36%	1.3x
$75,000 - $99,999	11%	1.4x
$100,000 - $149,999	6%	1.4x
$150,000 or more	4%	1.4x

Wired Magazine recently did a survey and discovered that 60% of Facebook users surveyed no longer knowing 20% of their friends there. 50% percent of those surveyed also stated that they only speak with about 20% of their friends on Facebook. That is perhaps why Mashable has many profiles on Facebook and an app that attracts over 190,000 users every month as well.

The many Mashable Facebook pages include:

Mashable - Tech (Technology Website)

Mashable - Business (Business News and Media)

Mashable - Social Media (Social Media News and Media)

Mashable - Startups (News and Media)

Mashable - Media (Media Website)

Mashable - Jobs (Job Locating Website)

Mashable - Follow (Links each of the sites one follows onto one tab)

Mashable - France (Personal Blog Site)

Mashable - Web Video (News and Media)

Mashable - HQ (Features its headquarters on Park Avenue, NY, NY)

Mashable App (The Latest in Digital, Social & Tech)

TWITTER

Twitter created 572,000 new accounts in one day back on March 12, 2011 (daily average is 460,000 new accounts). Some online stats display 600 million active Twitter users that spend around 12 minutes per visit and tweet an average of 340 million tweets per day.

Of course it would make sense that Mashable would promote their programs through this social media platform as well. Pete Cashmore is the author of Mashable tweets. Pete tweets nearly non-stop every day adding new tweets almost on an hourly basis. He uses Twitter primarily because it offers Mashable the opportunity to post short and to the point updates.

Who is the audience on Twitter? The number of male users is greater than the number of female users as per Google AdPlanner. They are 55% male to 45% male respectively. More than 70% of Twitter subscribers are between the age of 25 and 54, with 42% earning annually between $25k and $50k.

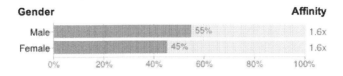

Gender .... **Affinity**

Male	55%	1.6x
Female	45%	1.6x

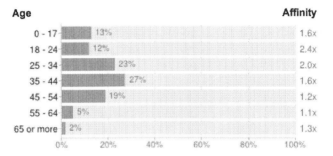

Age .... **Affinity**

0 - 17	13%	1.6x
18 - 24	12%	2.4x
25 - 34	23%	2.0x
35 - 44	27%	1.6x
45 - 54	19%	1.2x
55 - 64	5%	1.1x
65 or more	2%	1.3x

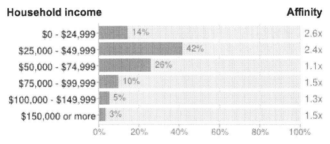

Household income .... **Affinity**

$0 - $24,999	14%	2.6x
$25,000 - $49,999	42%	2.4x
$50,000 - $74,999	26%	1.1x
$75,000 - $99,999	10%	1.5x
$100,000 - $149,999	5%	1.3x
$150,000 or more	3%	1.5x

Mashable generally includes in their tweets links to fresh content relevant to their audience. They monitor 'hashtags' to find the people following a certain topic and they post questions to their audience in a one-on-one interactive conversation.

LINKEDIN

LinkedIn currently has more than 160 million users. On LinkedIn Mashable display to their followers their expertise as the largest independent website dedicated to news, information and resources. Mashable updates its LinkedIn Company Profile several times per month.

Who is the LinkedIn audience? 55% of LinkedIn subscribers are male. Nearly 80% are between the age of 25 and 54 and 10% between the age of 55 and 64 or older (see below demographics from Google AdPlanner). On LinkedIn, Mashable can choose to share content with all their followers or just with members of a specific group.

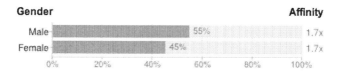

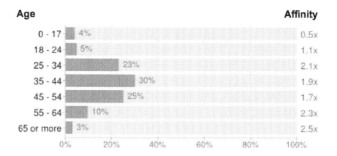

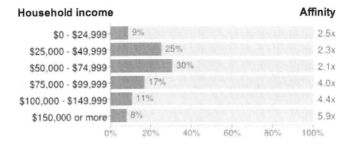

Household income		Affinity
$0 - $24,999	9%	2.5x
$25,000 - $49,999	25%	2.3x
$50,000 - $74,999	30%	2.1x
$75,000 - $99,999	17%	4.0x
$100,000 - $149,999	11%	4.4x
$150,000 or more	8%	5.9x

GOOGLE+

Google has been recently very busy launching innovations to all of their platforms and Mashable covers them all.

Mashable was one of the first brand to join Google+ and uses itfor a variety of reasons specific to the platform. A key element of Google+ is that it focuses on 'targeted sharing' with subsets within social groups or 'Circles'. Mashable updates its Google+ profile almost daily. Another crucial element within Google+ is its section specifically devoted to viewing, editing and managing multimedia. Using the photo tab, users can view all of the photos posted including the ones they are 'tagged' in. Google+ has an image editor similar to Instagram and there are privacy options and sharing features to select from. Google's more recent group chat feature, 'Hangouts' is another very useful tool for interacting with a community and distributing the video recordings to YouTube. Mashable has used it as a virtual meeting to connect with its employees and also as a multi-person video chat tool to connect with their audience. For more details on how Mashable uses Google+, watch Meghan Peters, Community Manager at Mashable (http://bit.ly/NjwhfT).

Google+ has over 100 million users, adding over 625,000 new users daily. It is ideally suited for starting conversations and adding people to them. The majority of Google+ users are male (69.62%). They include Marketing professionals, Web designers, Engineers, Software developers and Students.

MASHABLE FOLLOW

Mashable Follow is an attempt to develop what they have called a new "Social Layer". In their own words, Mashable Follow moves the company from being purely editor-driven to becoming a news community encouraging its readers to become engaged in the news process. They are accomplishing this through 'Curation' that empowers their followers to choose what news is more important to them.

With Mashable Follow you can:

Find And Follow Your Favorite Topics: browse the most popular topics or search for specific topics and then click on the 'Follow' button accompanying each story to be notified every time a new story matching your topic is posted.

Share Stories To Your Favorite Networks: with the 'M Share' button, all of your social media buttons (Facebook, Twitter, Google Buzz and Digg accounts) are incorporated in a single one that allows social sharing across multiple platforms at once.

Connect And Interact With Other People Sharing The Same Interests As You: by creating a Profile on Mashable Follow (use your Facebook or Twitter logins to connect), you will be able to follow and interact with other users that share the same interests as you.

Currently Mashable has over 3,000 stories posted on their site and more than 14,000 followers on their Mashable Follow. Every story is preceded by a compelling visual image and followed by the subtabs where readers can connect the stories to their Facebook, Twitter, Google+, Linkedin, Pinterest and StumbleUpon accounts.

YOUTUBE

10.35% of Mashable traffic in June 2012 was driven through YouTube as compared to 22.28% from Facebook (source: Alexa.com). So it would make sense for Mashable to consider the traffic variance while working with these two different social media platforms.

Top Queries from Search Traffic

The top queries driving traffic to mashable.com from search engines. Updated monthly.

	Query	Percent of Search Traffic
1	facebook	22.28%
2	youtube	10.35%
3	twitter	1.66%
4	you tube	1.42%
5	mashable	1.40%
6	pinterest	0.89%
7	amazon	0.67%
8	zerg rush	0.60%
9	face book	0.55%
10	gmail	0.54%

Mashable has currently over 25,000 subscribers to their YouTube pages that have made more than 18,500,000 views on YouTube. Mashable knows that creating a YouTube account is easy. The real task lies in building the channel for their brand. It is not enough to simply have a presence, but they strive to become a 'destination' by standing out to its viewers; after all there are more than 4 billion views on YouTube every day. They do so by dealing with three main aspects of using YouTube: comment moderation, new and relevant video content, and aesthetics.

Mashable updates their YouTube page daily in order to draw people back to their channel. They show an average of nine or ten new videos daily. They also remind viewers of new activity by syncing their YouTube content with their other social networks. On Mashable.com there is an entire section dedicated to videos.

In addition to linking their YouTube channel to their website, on YouTube Mashable attempts to optimize their videos to attract traffic from the search engines by listing titles containing targeted keywords and detailed descriptions. They also include these keywords in the 'tags' field of all the articles they post. All this makes it easier for viewers to find Mashable videos via the search engines.

One successful method Mashable deploys to attract attention to their videos is posting popular content. A good example of this is the video they posted about Microsoft's 'Surface

Tablet'. With this video, posted on June 19th, Mashable leveraged the attention that has been focused on the latest technology duel between Microsoft and Apple. The video has attracted over 1,000 views in the first 10 days.

PINTEREST

Pinterest is evolving so quickly that it is difficult to identify any one approach to using it as being *the* best method. Businesses such as Mashable are doing many things on Pinterest to promote their presence and attract followers to their site. Let's take a look at some of the most effective strategies they employ at the moment.

There are 422 articles about Pinterest currently displayed on the Mashable Social Media channel at Mashable.com. Find them by typing 'Pinterest' in the search box on their site. It takes my browser fifteen pages to list them all. On their Pinterest profile, Mashable currently has 41 boards, 700 pins and nearly 38,000 followers. All this shows that Mashable is definitely interested in this topic.

The vast majority of the things Mashable pinned onto their Pinterest boards are from their own website. However some of their pins are pinned or repinned from other sources as well. Take the 'Pinsanity! – when the Pinterest addiction goes a little too far' video for example. Mashable pinned this video from YouTube.com.

Pete Cashmore, founder and former CEO of Mashable has two personal profiles on Pinterest. One of them is based in France and the other one is out of San Francisco. On his San Francisco page, Pete has started an interactive Pinterest collaboration as an experiment for anyone who has a favorite SXSW experience. So far it had 225 pins.

One of the most recent boards created by Mashable is titled 'The More You Know' and features a few pins to date. One of them is a video concerning how McDonald's uses Photoshop to enhance product images used in its advertisements. When you click on the pin you can see from the information below the image that it was originally pinned by Mashable from their website, mashable.com. In its first hour the pin has been repinned twelve times, had four 'likes' and a couple of comments. The video link takes the viewer back to the Mashable website.

These are a few examples that just scratch the surface of how Mashable uses Pinterest to pin memes and various other web-culture, along with gadgets from the world of digital technology. They do this in unison with their self-proclaimed mission to tell the story about the "importance of digital innovation" and to relate how such "empowers and inspires" people from all around the world.

They also attempt to do so through the power of crowdsourcing whenever people repin their images and by using their 'Follow' button on all their corresponding pages. Another thing Mashable does very well, which is very Pinterest oriented, is hosting contests. The 'Mashable Photo Challenge' is one example. This board invites readers to follow particular prompts that are weekly submitted on their 'Challenge Page' thus attracting many people to their web pages.

These examples illustrate how Mashable uses various Social Media platforms in ways that are specific to each one. The content, pages and information that Mashable creates and curates are most of the time duplicated across all of these platforms. Ultimately however, all of their pages throughout the various networks lead people back to their main domain - Mashable.com. This is their primary goal and they do it very well.

As we seen so far there is no social network platform that made it through to the top charts and where Mashable is not yet present. In the next chapters we will be discussing one by one some of these big social media platforms out there providing you with the top tips and resources for a better online social experience.

2

Are You On Facebook?

Facebook is a social networking platform, already translated into more than 70 languages that businesses cannot afford to overlook. To date there are more than 900 million active users on Facebook (55% of the world's online audience is on Facebook) from more than 200 countries (see table on the next page from zoomsphere.com showing the top 15 countries on Facebook).

About 65% of the businesses worldwide are leveraging this platform. For marketers and businesses, Facebook offers an affordable and easily accessible tool for improving brand visibility, engaging customers and increasing online traffic.

	Country name	Users
1.	United States	155,707,900
2.	Brazil	51,172,180
3.	India	49,807,020
4.	Indonesia	43,831,880
5.	Mexico	35,602,820
6.	Turkey	31,112,380
7.	United Kingdom	30,640,560
8.	Philippines	28,262,700
9.	France	24,300,860
10.	Germany	23,742,040
11.	Italy	21,926,160
12.	Argentina	19,034,960
13.	Canada	17,633,400
14.	Colombia	16,825,380
15.	Spain	16,241,800

KISS Metrics have recently done some research and found that:

the best day to share on Facebook is Saturday

the best time to post is at noon (EST)

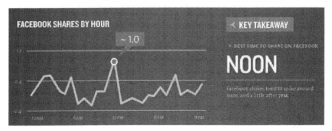

and one post every two days will help you get more 'likes'.

Visibli.com also provided some very interesting stats about Facebook 'Likes'. They say that 50% of the Facebook posts receive their 'Likes' within the first 80 minutes of being published, 80% within the first 7 hours and 95% within the first 22 hours.

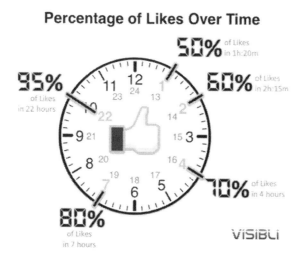

Setting Up Facebook For Business

There are several different types of accounts that can be created on Facebook and I've listed them below:

Profile Account: for individuals, solopreneurs or writers. Here you have the option to 'become friends' with someone or 'subscribe' to their content and decide how much of this content enters your stream. The average Facebook user has 130 friends and is connected to around 80 pages, groups or events.

Business or Fan Pages: for different types of businesses including local businesses. This is the type of page that will be discussed in great detail in this book. Note that fans rarely visit a page once they've 'Liked it' and they do not usually see what other fans have posted. If fans didn't interact with a Business Page for a while, they will stop seeing updates from that Page. It has been proved that posts on Pages with more than 1 million Fans are seen on average by 2.79% of those Fans. So it's your duty as a Community Manager to always find creative ways to engage your fans.

Group or Community Pages: these pages are maintained by the community together with the admin (the group creator). Every time someone adds a new post or comment, everyone in the community is notified by email. 'Group Members must be approved or added by other members' and as a group administrator you may set up an email address so people in the group can post on the move.

Places or Check-in Pages: an opportunity for local businesses to promote deals and increase their customer base. This type of page can be merged with a Business Page and we will discuss this type later in this book.

As we discussed different types of accounts, I thought it is worth mentioning a great article from Facebook itself highlighting '**The Different Kinds Of Facebook Users**': The Lurker, The Hyena, The Mr/Ms Popular, The Gamer, The Prophet, The Thief, The Cynic, The Collector, The Promoter, The Liker, The Hater, The Anti-Proofreader, The Drama Queen/King, The News, The Rooster, etc. Read it to find out which type are you.

Creating Facebook Business Pages has different requirements from the personal profile or other types of accounts. While a personal profile is limited to 5000 friends, a business page can have an unlimited number of fans. To get started, you need to register your business.

Go ahead to http://facebook.com/pages and choose a suitable category for your business page. There are six categories to choose from including 'local business or place', 'company, organization or institution', 'brand or product', 'artist, band or public figure', 'entertainment' or 'cause or community'. If you are a local business, it is beneficial to categorize your business as 'local' as this will allow it to appear in regional directories.

After picking the category, proceed to name your page and then tick the box that indicates that you have permission to create a page for your business. This will lead you to a page template profile for your business. You can customize this page to your liking by following the instructions on the interface.

Next, create starter messages that will get other users to 'Like' your page. For your starter messages, offer your target audience information that is interesting and valuable. This can be in the way of tips on how they can use your product to do something more efficiently or faster. You can also create an entertaining video tutorial, or upload a webcast. However, as you get started, do not sell your product too much as this will turn off those that you are trying to get to 'Like' your page.

Invite people in your personal network including friends, colleagues and family to 'Like' your page by using the 'Suggest To Friends' tab. To personalize your Facebook business page URL, go to http://facebook.com/username. You'll need to provide your cell phone number to receive a confirmation code that activates your chosen URL. Think through your username before creating and securing it, because you will not be able to change it later.

Facebook offers you the ability to customize your business pages to reflect your brand. The landing page is important. Create one that will appeal to your target audience and will distinguish you from the competition.

Wall posts are a great addition to feature on your business pages. This platform allows your target audience and customers to tell their opinion about your products and services. Encourage this type of interaction by clicking on the 'Friends can post on my wall' and 'Can comment on posts setting' to enable the 'Everyone' setting.

Facebook Timeline And Competitive Analysis

Facebook introduced the 'Timeline' feature (defined by Zukerberg as 'The Story Of Your Life In One Page') on March 30 2012, which replaced the Wall. The new Timeline feature allows online marketers and businesses to display information about what they are up to, over a given period. With this feature, other users get to know more about your business as time passes by.

Below I've listed the main features of the new Facebook Business Page:

Timeline Cover Photo: needs to be 851x315 pixels and can't include any kind of advertising such as price, contact details or calls-to-action. Check '20 Facebook Page Cover Photos To Inspire Your Brand' from Mashable to see some examples.

Picture Photo: needs to be 180x180 pixels and you can upload a logo, a photo of yourself or a product image.

About Section: you can add a description of up to 160 characters; URLs preceded by 'http://' are clickable. If you are a 'local business' this section is automatically filled with your business address, telephone number and opening hours. However if you want to show your site instead of the telephone number for example, I suggest you select 'no phone' in the Basic Information section and introduce your website address in the website field.

Application Boxes or Tabs: you can have up to 12 including your 'Likes' and 'Photos'. Note that only 'Photos' can't be moved, the rest of the application boxes can be re-arranged based on your priorities. The first four boxes will show without clicking on the down arrow. In the Application boxes, as shown in the examples on the next page, you can have tabs such as: welcome or home, why 'Like' us?, house rules, a call-to-action such as 'sign up to our emails, 'download now the latest report about…' or 'contact me', a link to your other social media accounts, testimonials or case studies, fan of the week, shop now, events, resources, FAQ, tutorials, videos, gift registry, etc.

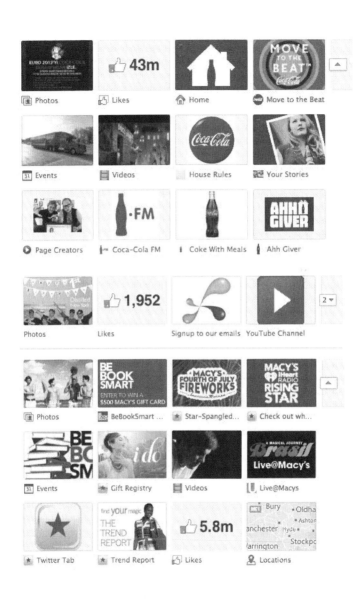

To change the cover or the name of one of the application boxes, click on the down arrow and then hover over the box you want to change until the pencil icon appears. Then click on 'Edit Settings'.

Posts: you have a maximum of 63,206 characters to tell your story in each post. By clicking on the star next to your post, you can expand it to the entire length of the page. By clicking on the pencil icon, you can hide it from your timeline or 'Pin (it) to Top'.

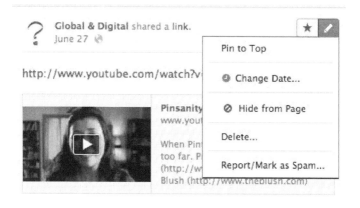

Milestones: add past events to your timeline such as product or book launches or even recording the day when you reached a certain number of fans.

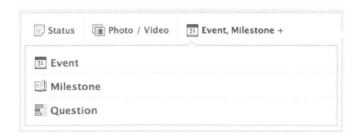

Competitive Analysis: Facebook Timeline also offers access to important metrics about your competitors. You can easily analyze your competition by simply going to their page, and then clicking on the 'Likes' application box. You will be able to view metrics such as the number of 'Likes', 'Talking about this', their 'Most popular week' and the 'Most popular age group' (see below insights for the Google Facebook page). Note that you can only analyze your competition if their Timeline feature is enabled and they too can spy on you if yours is enabled.

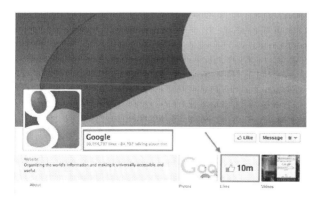

There are various metrics to measure when analyzing how well your competitors are leveraging Facebook. You can make use of the **Talking About This** feature. This tells you about the number of Likes, Shares and Comments your competition's page received. If the fans are active and loyal, it means that they are more engaged with that business.

Another metric that you could analyze using the Timeline feature is the **Engagement Rate: compute this by dividing the 'People Talking About This' value by the 'Total Likes'.** This metric offers you insights into the rate of engagement per fan. If the value is high, it means that the fans that are engaging on that page are high quality. There are online studies that show that since the Timeline was launched there is a 13% increase in fan engagement and a 46% in content engagement. Check the 'More Facebook fans equals lower engagement rates' article from prdaily.com for more details on engagement rates by brand.

You may also take a different angle of analysis by using the **trend line** to track the main events happening across a specific time. This may assist you in determining why fan interaction was higher at a given time. Also, make use of the **Most Popular Week** feature as it tells you the main events and highlights of your competition in a certain week. To access this data you need to click on the 'Likes' box.

Acquiring Facebook Fans

Active Facebook fans are the backbone of your Facebook presence. There are numerous techniques to use in acquiring active Facebook fans and we shall only discuss a few here. Some statistics show that brands are acquiring fans at a rate of 9% per month.

A good place to start is by building an appealing canvas or landing page. Include a video explaining what your fan page entails, whom it is created for and why users want to become fans. This approach enables you to convert page visitors into fans.

Consider adding a link to your Facebook fan page in the emails that you send out to business associates, customers, friends, family and colleagues. This will save you the effort of constantly promoting your personal profile and instead actively driving attention to your business pages. You can also promote it on Twitter a couple of times a week. See some examples below on how others do it.

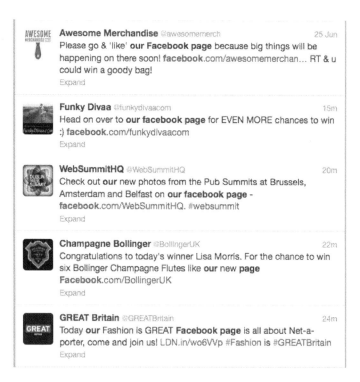

Make good use of photos especially if your business usually hosts live events. Post these photos on your fan page and ask your existing fans to tag themselves. This approach provides you with relevant and free exposure as your content appears in your fans' News Feed and that of their friends.

Also, consider using text messaging to ask users to join you. This is especially effective when you are just starting out and looking to build your fanbase. To join your fan page through text messaging, users need first to register for Facebook text messages. On their mobiles, inside the Facebook app they need to follow the following steps: Settings>Text Messaging>Activate Facebook Text Messages>Choose Your Country>Choose Your Network Provider>Send a text with the message 'fb' to 32665>Enter confirmation code. Once this is done they can send a text message such as 'fan **PageName**' to like a certain fan page. This approach is more practical if you are hosting a live event and if users have a smartphone with them.

Another way to increase your fan base is to make use of social plug-ins and widgets (http://developers.facebook.com/docs/plugins/) such as the 'Like Box' or the 'Facepile' on your business blog or website. It is also a good idea to include a title box just on top of the Like box to allow site visitors to click on the 'Like' button to become your Facebook Fans.

Facebook Community Management

As your business grows, you might want to hire a community manger to help you with the continuous management of the community on Facebook. An effective community management strategy ensures that your brand remains constructively engaged with your fans.

An important aspect of community management entails responding to the questions asked by the fans. Even when you do not have answers to all the questions, it is important that you make a consistent effort to offer relevant replies. Check that your notification alerts are turned on for you to receive fan emails in your inbox after publishing a post.

As a community manager, you play the role of a moderator. You want to ensure that fans feel safe and comfortable posting on your wall. As such, guarantee the safety of your fans as they communicate with you. Be open to constructive criticisms instead of reacting negatively to it; this will keep fans from feeling free to have a conversation with you.

As a moderator, it is also your role to be on the lookout for spam messages. Feel free to delete these, as they do not add value to your Facebook conversation with your genuine fans. Act as a neutral moderator when the conversation becomes too contentious.

As part of the community management on Facebook, you might want to set out ground rules as fans interact with each other on your platform. Of course, you do not want the rules to be too stringent to allow free flowing conversation. However, make the rules clear and visible to all the fans by placing them in the information area or on a separate window.

While you do not have to sit around engaging your fans all day long, a good approach to take is to set daily a given amount of time for community management on Facebook.

Top 13 Facebook Apps

There are a lot of Facebook apps that developers put at our disposal, however the ones I found more useful for small businesses and startups are listed below:

1. NetworkBlogs: imports your most recent blog posts onto your timeline

2. Fan Of the Week or **Booshaka:** every week one of your fans that interacted with your page is chosen to be the 'fan of the week'

3. TubeMogul: distributes your videos to several video sites at once (including YouTube) and also loads these videos onto your Facebook Business Page

4. MailChimp: this tool allows you to add a newsletter signup form to your Facebook Business Page. It is free for up to 2,000 subscribers and 5,000 mailings

5. iFrame Wrapper or Static iFrame App: this tool allows you to add a welcome page or any other pages to your Facebook Business Account. Although your Timeline is your landing page, you can add a 'welcome page' and list it as an app box just beside your 'Photos'. Note that each page you create will have a unique URL, however the organic traffic will always land on your Timeline.

6. SurveyMonkey or Poll Daddy: make use of these tools if you want to create surveys and polls

7. WildFire App: allows you to organize contests or promotional events. Please note that only big advertisers can run contests directly on Facebook, everyone else needs to use an app. For promoting events you can also use **EventBrite**

8. Scribd For Pages or **SlideShare**: allow people to view and download your documents/ebooks from Scribd/SlideShare directly from your Timeline

9. Ecwid or Payvment: add a store to your Facebook Page. These apps are integrated with Paypal, Google Checkout and Authorize.net

10. MyWebees: helps you get your entire site on Facebook

11. RSS Graffiti: allows feeding fresh content from different sources onto your Facebook Page

12. Review, OpenTable or Zagat: collect ratings and reviews

13. Livestream: live events streamed directly onto your Business Page

Mastering Facebook Ads

Before discussing this topic, I would like to invite you to read online a great article, called 'Do Facebook Ads Bring Customers?', that provides real examples of start-ups and small businesses using Facebook advertising. It is said that Facebook ads are more targeted and four times cheaper than AdWords, however they provide less direct sales. See below a comparative table done by searchenginejournal.com.

AdWords vs Facebook Ads

Channel	AdWords	Facebook Ads
Keywords	Yes	No
Likes	No	Yes
Demo	Limited	Accurate, Extensive
Geo	Yes	Yes
Avg Cost	$2.50 CPC	$0.80 CPC

The first step in mastering Facebook ads is to **Think Carefully About Your Audience And Decide What To Promote:** your Page or a post on your Page? an event? an app? or a website outside Facebook? See below examples of different Facebook ads.

Philips HomeLiving UK

Busy mums need a helping hand sometimes, so 'like' us for family recipes and giveaways!

👍 Like · 25,578 people like this.

Marketing Talks Live

Want to know what types of content are most compelling? Join us on June 28th. RSVP today!

📅 Join · 925 people are going.

Track Everything Social
business.ubervu.com

Actively monitor and filter conversations on Twitter, Facebook, blogs, news sites and more

Facebook allows you to select the type of audience you want your ads to target. Your business ads can target users based on their gender, location, age, interest, and relationship status. You may also decide to target those who are already fans of your business pages or fans in your personal network of friends. Alternatively, you can target your advertisement to reach users who have certain words in their profiles or in their status messages. By narrowing your ads to target a specific group you will be in a better position to maximize your advertising budget and improve your return on investment. However be sure not to narrow your target audience too much as you might risk leaving out other eligible groups.

As you start to create an ad campaign on the Facebook platform (facebook.com/advertising), the default setting is advertising in a destination outside Facebook. Change this to the 'I want to advertise something I have on Facebook' option. When you advertise within the Facebook platform, users can like the page within the ad itself. With this later option, users can connect and actively engage with your page without clicking through the ad. Since June 2012, Facebook ads and sponsored stories also show on Zynga.com to everyone logged in with their Facebook account.

Mastering The Click-Through-Rates: Another factor to consider in managing your Facebook ads is the click-through

–rate (CTR=number of clicks/number of times your ad is shown). Facebook determines how successful your ads are by considering the CTR that the ads generate. Facebook gives more visibility and lower cost-per-impression or cost-per-click for ads with high CTR. Be sure to keep your CTR at a certain threshold, preferably over 0.1, as anything below this rate will signal a poor performing ad.

Nevertheless, you need to continuously test the performance of your ads to determine their effectiveness. If your ads CTR fall below 0.1, for example, you want to create a new ad because it is difficult to improve the ad performance at this point.

Utilizing The 'Friends Of Connections' Feature: This feature can prompt the friends of those already in your network to view the ads on their page. Friends are more likely to check out a page if they see that their friends have done the same. While the 'Friends of Connection' feature allows you to leverage your network, it can also limit the advertisement impressions. However if you are looking to target a narrow group with your ads, then this feature may come in hand. Some ads will perform better with this feature than others. A good approach to take is to test how effective the 'Friends of Connections' Feature is with each ad campaign that you create.

Making Sense Of Actions: An action takes place when a user Likes your ad, but does not click through to your business pages. Other actions could be: shares and comments on specific posts, credits spent and apps use.

It is challenging to measure the cost per fan on Facebook ads. However, Facebook offers extra reports to allow you to estimate the cost and conversion metrics involved in generating fans. One of these reports is the 'Advertising Performance' report, which provides you insights into how well you are leveraging the advertising platform.

Daily Budget vs. Daily Spending Limit: To master Facebook ads, you need to consider the amounts you are spending on your ad campaign. Start by distinguishing between the daily budget and the daily spending limit. The 'daily budget' is the amount you want to spend daily on one campaign. The 'daily spend limit' is the ceiling Facebook places on your account which is automatically placed at $50 daily. If you want to expand your daily spend limit to reach a wider audience, you might want to contact Facebook and ask them to change your daily spending limit. Otherwise

Facebook will automatically increase this if they see that you pay regularly what you've spent.

You need to keep creating new ads, tweaking and testing them. This way you will know what is working and what is not worth the investment. To end this subchapter I would like to provide a brief summary on a campaign I run for one of my local clients so you know what to expect when running a Facebook ad campaign with a small budget. The client had a budget of $50 and we prepared 5 ads (directing to their fan page) that were shown to about 9,000 Facebook users. This campaign brought 136 clicks at a CTR of 1.51% and about 75 fans. So the cost per fan came to 66 cents.

Facebook Contests And Sweepstakes

Facebook contests and sweepstakes are a great way of engaging your fans and prospective clients. These contests allow you to reward fans in exchange for Liking your pages. However, Facebook has stringent regulations regarding how companies host these contests.

Facebook restricts the hosting of any contests, collection and judging of fan entries and announcing of winners on your business pages. You risk having your accounts suspended if you engage in any of these practices. You can host contests on your Facebook page directly if you buy at least $10,000 worth of ads in three months.

Facebook allows you to host promotions and contests for example if you state 'Like our page to enter the promotion'. This option requires you to provide an application that will cater for the registration process. Alternatively, you may host a contest outside of Facebook, for example by stating, 'Like our page and enter the promotion by registering on our company website'.

Purchasing ads worth $10,000 can be too costly for many businesses. However, you can use third party applications to create a micro-site for hosting the contest. These applications also allow you to integrate the micro-site with Facebook so that users can Like your business pages or share the contest details with their own friends. Most of the applications allow you to embed a contest widget in your Facebook pages FB so that visitors are directed to the micro-site from Facebook.

Effective contest platform providers to use include Votigo, Wildfire, and Strutta. These apps allow you to create customized entry forms, accept entries in any format including text, video and photos and allow people to vote on entries within a single platform. One benefit of using these apps is that Facebook offers you reports on the contest activities in addition to traffic reports. Most contest platform providers charge about $10 each month for their services.

Facebook Commerce

Selling on the Facebook platform is also known as F-commerce. You can conduct f-commerce:

a) by displaying your products on your Facebook page and then re-directing people to your site to complete the purchase

b) or integrate your complete shopping system onto Facebook

Facebook-Initiated Selling: Fans can look through your Facebook storefront for the products/services you are offering. Then, when they click through to buy one of the displayed products, they are directed to a site where they can complete the shopping process.

Complete Selling On Facebook: Companies such as Delta Airlines have created complete stores and online shopping systems (Delta Ticket Counter) on their Facebook pages. The complete selling option allows you to build a full store on Facebook without directing users elsewhere. You may also enable users to post messages about your company or product offering on their walls and to share details of the product offering with friends.

Some of the best Third party solutions or applications that you can use to enable f-commerce for your business include SortPrice, Useablenet, StoreFrontSocial, and Payvement. At the end of June 2012, Facebook decided to remove their 'Credits' system and replace them with a 'subscription billing' where the company will be getting 30% in royalties.

Facebook Check-in Deals

Facebook Check-in Deals allow you to reward customers who come to your local storefront. This is especially important as local businesses seek to attract local customers who are not only smart phone savvy but are also on the lookout for local deals. Facebook also tried the Groupon model of 'daily deals' and decided to end it, as it wasn't a sustainable model. In Groupon's case, they have to recruit the businesses to advertise in the daily deals and negotiate the best deals possible, which sometimes do not bring any profit to the advertiser. In the Facebook model, individual businesses are uploading themselves all the details of the offer they would like to promote (see video instructions at facebook.com/deals/checkin/business) and Facebook just provides the platform and take a cut of the earnings. Since August 2011, Facebook users can tag status updates, photos or videos with a location so businesses can then create promotions for people that checked-in at their location.

To get started with Facebook Check-in Deals, you either need to create it or claim it from Facebook if there is one already created. Note that a Facebook Places Page is different from a Facebook Business Page or a Group Page. A Facebook Places Page usually has a map and a list of people that already checked-in at that location. The different types of business pages someone could create on Facebook confused many people, so Facebook now gives the option to merge a Facebook Business Page with a Facebook Places Page (see Disneyland Facebook Places Page below). Once you've claimed your Places Page you should have a link on that page that says 'Merge with existing page'.

Disneyland
14,562,232 likes · 197,999 talking about this · 2,225,761 were here

Travel/Leisure
Welcome to the official Facebook Page of the Disneyland Resort! Learn about Park updates, news, and special backstage info here.

About

Photos   Let The Memo...

Events   Map

To create a Places Page you need to be at the location and 'Check-In'; add a description and tag friends (see below instructions from Facebook).

To create a new location, use a mobile device with location services enabled:

1. Tap ▦
2. Select ⚇ **Nearby**
3. Tap **Check In** (top-right corner)
4. Tap the plus sign (+) in the top-right corner
5. Type the name and an optional description for the location you want to add
6. Tap **Add**

You can then continue to post from the location:

1. Write a caption, tag friends or add a photo
2. Tap **Post**

Then go to Facebook and search for the Place you just added. Then claim the page as your business by clicking on 'Know the owner?' tab.

Next, Facebook will ask you for your business email address or a document displaying your business name. This allows Facebook to establish the existence of your business and it may take up to a week before you receive a confirmation.

After your request is granted, create a deal by selecting the 'Create Deal' tab to the left on the 'Edit Page' (see video

instructions   at
http://facebook.com/deal/checkin/business). A splash
page will appear where your deal will be displayed once you
create one. Then, select a deal type from the individual deal,
friend deal, loyalty deal and charity deals. Remember to place
restrictions on your deal such as the duration of the deal or
the quantity that a customer can redeem. After this, you
need to wait for Facebook to review and approve your deal
before you can promote it. It usually takes up to 48 hours
until your deal is approved. Note that offers are free to
create and free to redeem.

You may promote your deal by placing it on your Facebook
Places page by selecting the 'Share With Connections' tab.
You may also promote it with Facebook ads or you can tell
customers who visit your local store about the deal. They
can then visit your Places pages and claim the deals through
their smart phones.

Remember to track how customers are redeeming the deal.
You might have to manually track this, as Facebook does not
yet offer a tool for tracking redeemed deals.

Mastering Facebook EdgeRank

The EdgeRank Facebook algorithm is a feature that selects the content that appears in users' newsfeeds. EdgeRank aims to put you/your business into the newsfeeds of your fans thus allowing you greater engagement with them. EdgeRank takes into consideration:

a) The time frame between when you post and when users are online. This ensures that users have access to your latest posts.

b) The weight of a post and the effort put into creating it. Pictures and videos have more weight than a link or a quick status update.

c) The affinity, which involves the amount of time users have engaged with you or your brand and vice versa.

To get started, go to EdgeRank.com to determine your own EdgeRank. This tool will offer you insights into the EdgeRank of your business pages as well as the days when your rank is high or low.

Increase the affinity you have with your customers by triggering a reaction or a conversation. So instead of posting statements only, consider asking your fans a question accompanying your content. This allows your fans to reply and to offer insights, opinions and feedback about the posts and importantly, about your business.

Facebook Content Marketing

Content marketing on Facebook allows you to attract active fans by availing content that is compelling, interesting and valuable for them. Remember that your goal is to engage an active fan base rather than one-off fans. Active fans are those who frequently Like your posts, comment on them and share them with their own network. Active fans are those who will vote for your content so that it appears in the enviable 'Top News' position.

As you leverage content marketing on Facebook, ensure that after posting, you follow up with your fans. If they are asking questions, respond to these questions and acknowledge the comments that your fans post in response to your content. Additionally consider tagging other businesses and fans that might be relevant to your content marketing campaign. This technique keeps fans from feeling that you are being too pushy with your own content. By occasionally diffusing attention to others, you can still engage in subtle selling.

Also, do not overlook the small efforts such as frequently posting relevant status updates, or sharing links. This will help you build your brand gradually. For your content marketing efforts to be successful, make use of different media forms including videos, curated content, Facebook invitations, shout outs to other businesses or individuals (@BusinessPage or @individual) as well product photos.

In summary, <u>effective content marketing using Facebook involves</u>:

a) Dedication to bringing a human face to your brand; customers want to know that they are communicating with a fellow person and not an abstract brand.

b) Creativity in sending messages; content should largely be focused on the fans.

c) Direct and regular engagement with your fans and network.

d) Development of content that is relevant and seamlessly shareable.

e) Demonstration of courtesy and insight when interacting with fans.

How To Use Facebook Insights

Facebook insights provide you with metrics concerning various aspects of your Facebook experience. These include content metrics, user trends, demographics and growth. The information you obtain from Facebook Insights assists you in making improvements to better leverage this social networking platform.

There are two types of insights:

User Insights: these are the total numbers of likes, the number of active fans, new likes and dislikes, the sources of the Likes and referrers, number of page views, new page views and media interaction with your page.

Interactions Insights: these insights include the feedback to your posts containing comments, likes and daily impressions, discussions, wall and video posts, mentions as well as reviews.

Important metrics to measure are:

Monthly Fan Size Growth: this shows the number of active fans or those who Liked your page at the beginning of each month. This metric provides you insights into your fan growth patterns.

The Engagement Rate: this shows you how engaged your fans are with your page. By determining the rate at which fans are interacting with your posts, you can identify the type of discussion and posts that interest them the most.

Dislikes: as you receive more Likes on your pages you will inevitably incur attritions in the form of 'Dislikes'. To calculate the attrition rate use the formula Daily Dislikes or Unlikes/Daily Fan Count. This will provide you insight into the number of fans leaving your page.

Page Views: this shows you the number of fans who have returned to your page; more like return customers, which is always a good sign. You can identify the page views by subtracting the unique pages views from the total number of page views.

Mentions: this shows you the rate at which other users tag you in their pages or posts. This is an important metric because it is the easiest method for friends of your fans to access your page.

Tab views: this is a new insight on Facebook and shows you the traffic that each tab on your page attracts. Using this metric allows you to determine the tabs that are important to keep and those you might want to remove.

Have You Heard Of Instagram?

Now that Facebook owns Instagram, I thought to include this topic in here as well.

Instagram, with over 50 million users worldwide, is an instant photo-sharing mobile app that lets you share photos (that you took personally) on your other social networks such as Facebook, Twitter, Flickr and Tumblr.

What makes Instagram so special are the variety of **filters and borders** that come with the app. Before you take your photo (and even after) you can select the type of effect you'd like to give to your picture: vintage, shiny and bright, black and white, smoky and toasty touch, artistic, retro, etc. These filters can be found at the bottom of your screen (as in the examples on the next page) and by clicking on the arrow beside your camera icon. Another great feature is the **tilt-shift** (looks like a water droplet and can be found at the top left) that allows you to focus on certain areas of the picture, almost as if you were using a special SLR lens.

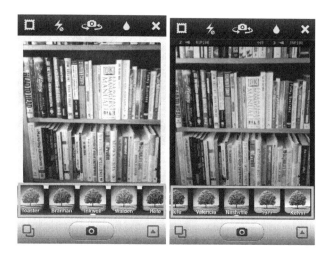

To upload a picture that you just took click on the green checkmark. Before sharing it with the world, you can also add a caption, a hashtag or @mention people. To return to the pictures view, click on the cross at the top left.

Creating an Instagram account is very easy. Just download the app from iTunes store if you have an iPhone or from Google Play if you have a smart phone powered by Android. Then log in with your Facebook or Twitter account details, upload a picture, write a 150-character description and include a URL to your site. You can choose to have a public or private account by switching off or on the 'Photos are private' option. You can also provide credentials for your other social networks, so pictures are shared automatically every time you post.

When using Instagram, you will notice a couple of icons:

The home icon: here you can see the latest pictures from people you follow (just like on Pinterest). Together with each photo, you may see 'likes' and comments.

The star icon: here you can see the most popular photos.

The camera icon: by tapping this icon, you'll be taken to a screen that allows you to take pictures just like I explained earlier.

The heart icon: here you can read the latest news about your followers and see who started following you.

The profile icon: this is the icon that brings you to your profile settings. Here you can search for friends to follow from your other social networks or just enter a username or a tag (hashtag) to search for other users to follow.

<u>You can leverage the power of Instagram by</u>:

a) sharing stunning pictures and liking other people's pictures

b) sharing pictures of your company, products, employees or customers

c) hosting contests where you ask your customers to take a picture of themselves with your product to win a prize

d) taking pictures at an event you organized and then @mention everyone when uploading the picture

Examples Of Businesses That Drive Traffic And Sales With Their Facebook Business Pages

Plenty of businesses are leveraging the power of Facebook to drive traffic and sales. A few examples include:

Macy's: a fashion retail shop largely relies on Facebook to attract customers to its ecommerce platform and to its physical storefront.

Petco: is a nationwide supply store for pets. The company, with local stores across the country, has seamlessly joined their stores with Facebook. This has allowed fans to spread the word and make recommendations to their friends about the products that Petco offers.

Toll Booth Saddle Shop: this local business deals with horse supplies in Philadelphia. It is a small business, but has a strong following on Facebook.

3

Are You Fun To Follow On Twitter?

Twitter, with more than 600 million global users (US 40% and International 60% from which Japan brings 40%, Spain 11%, UK 10% and Brazil 7%), offers a fantastic opportunity that most other social platforms and communication channels do not. This is both a micro-blogging and social networking site that allows businesses to find their customers, engage them and receive feedback in real-time. Tweets are indexed by Google so make sure you use the right keywords when promoting your business.

In the previous chapter, I mentioned a study done by KISS Metrics about the best time to post on Facebook. The same research also provided some interesting facts about Twitter.

KISS Metrics showed that:

80% of the US population is in the Eastern and Central Time Zones. So for maximum reach and effectiveness it is recommended that you post when more people are likely to be online and interact with your tweets. Check http://timeanddate.com for time conversion, if you are outside these time zones.

The best time to get re-tweeted is at 5pm EST.

For a high CTR (click-trough-rate) on your links it is recommended to tweet midweek and on weekends, around noon and 6pm EST and between 1 and 4 times per hour

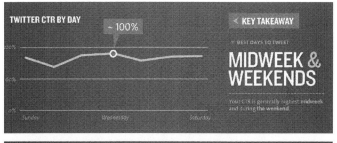

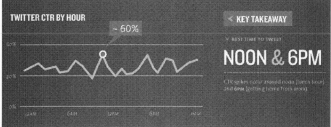

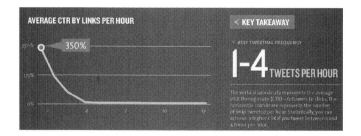

Using Twitter As A Communication Device

Twitter can be an effective tool to communicate and stay in touch with your audience. However, one mistake that businesses make is to use Twitter as a tool for dissemination of information only. While you can spread the word about your business and product offering, it is important that you actively engage with your audience. To use Twitter as a tool for communication you must first understand the needs of your target audience. This way, you will be informing and engaging them with messages that are relevant to them.

Self-promotion is an important element for any business. Nevertheless, do not make this the primary form of communication with your twitter audience. Share information that is both relevant to your business and your audience. Offer third party information such as outside resources and links, to establish credibility with your audience. As such, you will also attract greater engagement with people that matter including journalists and bloggers.

Be consistent in your communication with followers. Although there are no steadfast rules on how often you should update your Twitter account, make it frequent and relevant and your followers will be anticipating the next update. Leverage the 140 characters to build relationships with your audience by committing to communicate with them.

Searching For Local Tweets And Tweeters

Most Twitter users tweet about things, events and places that are in their location. For local businesses, this makes it easy to locate and interact with potential and existing local customers or business partners. You can use several methods to search for local tweets and tweeters including:

Find Local People With Your City In Their Profile: One method of finding local people in Twitter, is to check through their profiles for mentions of your city. Start by searching Twitter for the name of your city at the search box. This will display the current tweets with your city's name. Next, select the 'People' tab to view the people who have your city name in their profiles. Click on their account name and then follow them.

Use Twitter Advanced Search: The advanced search on Twitter allows you to include geography as you search for local people. Twitter allows you to find people tweeting within 1 to 1000 miles radius in a zip code or city. You will get varied results because the search displays only the most recent tweets. Look through the tweets that are displayed and then follow the people that interest you.

Use Twitter Grader: Twitter Grader helps you determine the quality of Twitter users before adding them to your community. This tool calculates users' grades ranging between 1 and 100 and displays the top 1000 users into the 'Twitter Elite' category. To get started, open the Twitter Grader (http://tweet.grader.com) and then look for people in a location, such as your city.

Use Twellowhood: The Twellowhood feature enables you to use the Twellow Twitter directory to find local people, based on where they are located. To get started, go to http://twellow.com/twellowhood and then type your location in the search box above the map. This tool allows you to view the Twitter users in your city. Look through the people displayed and choose those that you want to follow.

Getting In Touch With Journalists In Your Local Area

Using Twitter lists is an effective way of targeting your audience and reaching out to influential Twitter users such as local journalists. Twitter lists assist you to easily aggregate your target audience into a single interface.

Tools such as Listorious and Twellow, have made the process of aggregating lists of important people, easier. Listorious is a directory of people who matter in various areas such as marketing, media, technology, business, finance and food. You can view lists that are popular and the number of people who follow these lists. Listorious also allows you to search using keywords or tags. This is a great tool to use in narrowing down followers who are really interested in your product/service offering.

Getting Started on Listorious:

1. Use A Specific Keyword To Define Your Niche And Expertise: Launch the Listorious platform and type in your chosen keyword. Make it simple and specific to allow you to see exactly what people in this niche are talking about.

2. Carefully Select Your List: Listorious will display a list that is specific to your keyword. Choose just a few lists to follow and those that are related to your niche or an area you are interested in such as media. Choose lists that include professional people in your niche or a niche such as 'media' if you are looking to interact with a local journalist.

3. Follow The Targets: Now that you have selected your lists, start to follow the people who are following the lists. It is likely that you share industry interests with these people. This is also an effective way to find an informed audience. You can see who is following the lists when you access Twitter. Be sure not to follow every person who is following the list; keep the number to about 20 per day.

The main advantage of using Listorious is that it is easy to aggregate targets and followers who are specific to your niche. In this way, you can easily find journalists in your area or industry who might be interested in your type of business, thus gaining you publicity. This tool is free, and easy to use.

Getting Started with Twellow:

Twellow is like Yellow Pages for the Twitter network. It allows you to search for people and topics and makes use of geography in these searches. It also enables you to search the number of followers a person has.

Twellow is a great tool to use in building networks with the most influential people, who can generate good publicity for your business. It not only helps you to locate potential customers but also to find important professionals within your location.

To find people in your niche or those who might be interested in your niche such as local journalists, simply include a search keyword onto the Twellow platform. Make your search words and phrases simple and specific to generate more targeted results. To follow people you need to create an account by offering your Twitter login details.

Twellow provides you a list of people who match your search word and you get to choose whom to follow. To follow influencers in any given field, add the person with the greatest followership; this person is typically at the top of the list. If you are looking to communicate directly with influential people, look for those with about 100 followers. These people are more likely to reply to your tweets and build a relationship with you.

As in Listorious, be sure not to follow too many people to allow yourself to genuinely engage and connect with your Twitter community. Find active users and those who are interested in your niche.

Using TweetDeck To Manage Your Interactions On Twitter

TweetDeck by Twitter (http://tweetdeck.com) is a free desktop and mobile application that allows you to organize and manage your interactions on Twitter and other social networking platforms. The tool aggregates all the tweets, mentions and followers into columns that make it easy to manage them. You do not have to be online to distribute tweets when using TweetDeck.

To get started on TweetDeck, simply visit its homepage, sign up and integrate it with your Twitter account. Some of the great features that TweetDeck offers businesses to personalize tweets include:

Add Or Change Location: This feature allows you to select the geographical location of your business from Google Maps. A link to this location will then accompany your tweets.

Videos And Photos: This feature allows you to include rich media into your tweets to make them dynamic and interactive.

Video Recording Using Webcam: This feature allows you to use your computer webcam to capture and record videos and then add them to your tweets.

TweetShrink This Update: This feature lets you shorten your tweet. It does this by using Twitter slang words to make the update brief and accessible to your followers. Before sending the tweet, be sure to review the shortened status update.

Translate This Update: This allows you to send your tweets to a global audience that speaks different languages. You can choose the language you want your tweets to be translated to.

Recent Hashtags: This feature lets you reuse the hashtags in your recent updates, saving you time in creating new hashtags for your tweets.

Schedule This Update: This feature allows you to send tweets when you are not online. In this way, tweets can be sent at a specific time even if you are not available to manually post these tweets at that time.

Sending Instant Coupons

TwtQpon is a Twitter application that allows local businesses to easily create coupons and offer them to their customers and followers on Twitter. This tool has proved effective for several companies such as Dell in driving sales and gaining brand visibility across the social networking platform.

At no fixed charges, you can create coupons to reward loyal customers and anyone who follows you. You can create a wide array of coupons including Secret Coupons, Group Coupons, Twitter Coupons and Followers Coupons. Once you create the coupons, you may Tweet them to Twitter users only, email to your personal or professional network or send it to other social networking sites including Facebook and LinkedIn. When users click on the links, they are directed to the TwtQpon site to see the coupon and then to your business site where they can redeem it.

To get started with TwtQpon, go to the TwtQpon official website and select the 'Create a Coupon' tab. Then enter:

a) Your Twitter name, name and details of the coupon

b) Add your brand logo or product image

c) Enter a coupon code to make tracking easy

d) Include a link to your business website

e) Specify the date when the coupon expires

Asking For Feedback

Polling your customers and Twitter followers is an effective method of obtaining feedback about your product offering and importantly, your business. Polling on Twitter also allows you to engage with your followers as you can ask them for input on content, your product/service or business brand.

You can ask anything on your poll, but it is also important to show your customers that their answers are valued. As such, post the results of the poll and allow participants to see how their answers matched up to the other followers.

Tools such as Twtpoll make it extremely easy for you to engage with your followers and customers in this way. While this is not a free tool, it allows you to simply embed the widget in your status updates or twitter account to get the poll started. If you are looking to integrate your Twitter account with your business site where you can conduct the poll, Twtpoll makes this possible as well. Once you create the poll, you will gain access to a code to paste on your website or a URL to accompany your Twitter status updates.

Announcing Events

Twitter can be a great way to generate buzz for your events and make these events recurring, without the need to spend too much on event marketing. The best time to use Twitter for events is before and after the event. Using this social media tool before the event creates buzz and using it after the event engages participants for new ideas for upcoming events.

One way to use Twitter to announce your event is to use a hashtag (#) for your events in the tweets that you post. Encourage your audience/Twitter followers to use the event hashtags as they talk about it. Offer incentives for people to include your hashtag in their tweets for example by issuing giveaway prizes to a lucky follower who liberally uses your event hashtag. If you are hosting a big event, create an independent Twitter account for it; this creates credibility and serves as a helpline for customers with inquiries.

Be creative when using Twitter to announce and create buzz for your event. One way of doing this is by changing the form of the message when sending out the tweets. This will allow you to announce your event without annoying your followers or seeming too pushy. Inform followers about speakers, sponsors or ask them for input on how to make the event better. Then, ask your followers to share the event by re-tweeting.

Partnering With Other Businesses And Tweeting Each Other's Offers

As a small business, it can be difficult to establish a loyal following on any social networking platform, including Twitter. However partnering with other businesses can help you improve your brand visibility and attract audiences that are more loyal. So, consider cross promoting other businesses' products and services across the Twitter network. You can also tweet them any offers you may have and that may interest them; in this way, they can either buy into the offer or promote it to their own followers.

To get started in partnering with other businesses, look out for businesses that may have a similar audience as yours. Use the same strategies discussed above to find tweeters and tweets in your location. These strategies can also help you find other businesses that complement your own business.

Next, create a pitch and then approach potential business partners. You can contact them directly over email or phone call and explain to them the benefits of partnering with you and cross promoting each other. Consider attending business-networking gatherings to meet potential business partners.

Once a partnership is established, you and your business partner will use various methods to promote each other. You can tweet about each other's offers and events, you can use their hashtags in your tweets, and you can embed links to their sites or blogs for followers to access relevant resources and content.

Finding The Influencers In Your Industry And Contacting Them

Twitter is an effective tool for identifying prospects, monitoring their online behavior and interacting with them directly. You can use several methods and tools to find potential customers that are looking for the product/services that you are offering.

One approach is to look for prospects using keywords that target a subject matter. When you search for people based on their tweets for example, you are better placed to know what they are looking for. You can then follow them on Twitter and respond to their queries or create a need for your product or service. To call someone's attention (they receive an email notification), use the '@' sign. To tweet about a topic you think people may be interested, use the '#' symbol.

Alternatively, you can check out people's profiles or bios to see if they are part of or interested in the niche that you serve. As a business, you will benefit from knowing the users who mention your niche, as you can go ahead and create a need for the product or service that they may be looking for. Twitter allows you to communicate directly with the people that you are following. This makes it easy to follow up on any lead that shows interest in your product.

A great tool to use in managing your Twitter contact list on Twitter is HootSuite. This third party application allows you to manage content whether you have multiple accounts or a single one.

To get started on HootSuite, go to their site and then select 'Sign up Now'. Then integrate this application by connecting with Twitter. This integration will allow you to view the tweets sent by your followers, any mentions of your business or product offering. It also allows you to see the people who want to interact with you directly, what they are talking about and the types of conversations your followers want to have with you directly.

Spying On Your Competitors

Spying on your competitors provides you with insights into how well they are leveraging the Twitter platform. Competitive analysis also tells you who is following your competition, who your competition is following, the conversations that followers are having and where your competition is mentioned.

An effective and easy to use tool is Who Follows Whom. This tool allows you to not only find the influencers that your followers are following, but also those of your competitors. Who Follows Whom enables you to see the followers that you and your competition have in common.

With this information, you can find strategies to improve the quality of your followers to gain a competitive advantage over your competition.

Researching Trends

Tweetmeme is especially important for businesses looking to keep abreast with trends in their niche. Tweetmeme also offers a 'retweet' tab that allows readers to distribute content links to Twitter.

By signing up for this service, you will have access to relevant trending news and topics. Twitter then directs these newsfeeds to your business site for your consumption. You get to decide the type of trends you want information about.

Tweetmeme places tweets into categories such as entertainment, lifestyle, comedy, science, sport, business, world politics and technology. These categories are further broken down into narrower sub-channels, making it easy to follow those trends that are specifically relevant to your niche.

Tweetmeme can also help you in managing content. It filters out personal tweets that may not be helpful in your research. It keeps topics that are indirectly related to your niche from cluttering your site. This is also an effective tool for bookmarking sites and resources that are of interest to you.

You can place the retweet button on your site so that you can redistribute any information you find interesting, to your Twitter followers.

Using Twitter As A Tool For Customer Support

Twitter is a versatile tool for you to communicate with your customers in real time. As a business, you can use Twitter to offer impeccable customer service and to make your customers feel valued. The best thing about this social platform is that customers can make inquiries and air their grievances and you can attend to these immediately.

However, take into consideration that this is an online social network where issues tend to go viral, fast. Ensure that your customer service strategy is effective enough to keep discontent as low as possible, to keep followers from spreading negative information about your business.

A golden rule for Twitter customer support is to respond fast to customer inquiries or complaints. It is best if you can respond in less than five minutes. Be sure to answer questions with relevant replies and offer to help customers who have complaints about your brand or product/service offering.

In supporting your customers, you want to make the experience personal. Even though you are a business, it is better to bring a human face in your interaction with customers on Twitter. Personalize your Twitter profile by including your name and the names of those who manage your Twitter account. Also, end your tweets with an actual name instead of initial or no name at all. In place of a business logo, place an avatar of your face to enhance face-to-face engagement with your audience.

Make use of DMs (direct messages) in times of crisis such as when there are too many complaints or inquiries coming in. The primary goal here is to help as many customers as possible using a small amount of time. First, you can publish a public tweet explaining the problem. People will see this tweet first when they access your profile. Secondly, reply to mentions to avoid cluttering the Twitter stream with the replies to customer complaints and inquiries. Let your customers know how you will help them. If the problem is minimized or solved, then you can go back to addressing individual customers.

In addition to offering customer service to your existing customers, you can also offer support to those who are not yet your customers. You can do this by reaching out to people who are asking questions in your niche area or area of expertise. Tools such as InboxQ, TweetDeck and HootSuite allow you to find these customers, support them and in return generate new leads for your business.

Advertising On Twitter

Facebook already made $3 billion from advertising in 2011 and it seems that Twitter is now getting serious about advertising and plans to generate at least $1 billion in ad revenue before 2014.

There are several ways to advertise on Twitter, but only two options available for small businesses: 'Promoted Tweets', and 'Promoted Accounts'.

With Promoted Tweets, Twitter selects 5 tweets, from the ones you've already promoted to your followers, and then they show them on a pay-per-click basis (and if relevant) at the top of the search results (as below) or in the users' timeline. This selection is mostly based on recency and engagement and they can even include some of your retweets, which you may not like. With this type of advertising you can decide how much you want to spend daily and how much you'd like to pay-per-click. When you start advertising with Twitter, the minimum bid is $0.50 and it will adjust after a few days, based on your historical performance or ad engagement. Compared to Adwords where a CTR of 1%-3% is very easy to achieve, on Twitter you'll regularly see CTRs of 0.05%. Monitor daily your advertising results and make sure you remove the low performer tweets.

With Promoted Accounts, you get to show up in the 'who to follow' section (as below). This type of advertising will target users that follow similar accounts to yours. And you can specify what is your daily budget and how much you'd like to pay per follower. As on the promoted tweets model, the minimum bid is $0.50 and Twitter will recommend a maximum bid and an estimate of how many followers you could get daily for your budget.

Resources

To learn more about advertising on Twitter go to https://business.twitter.com/smallbiz/ and watch the video on that page and also download the pdf that Twitter has put at your disposal.

To read about companies that are driving results with Twitter advertising go to https://business.twitter.com/en/optimize/case-studies/.

Examples Of Businesses That Drive Traffic And Sales With Their Twitter Account

Dell Outlet: began using Twitter to distribute information about the deals they were offering. Within a short time, followers created buzz around these deals and the followership grew tremendously. Today Dell Outlet uses Twitter only a couple of times each week to update customers about any deals and to interact and engage with them about relevant topics. The department has been able to generate over $3 million in sales revenue, something that they attribute to their Twitter engagement. Their own research also indicates that Dell Outlet has gained greater brand visibility too.

Teusner Wines: is a high-end winery in Australia with just three employees. When the business began using Twitter, they made use of keywords to find users interested in the wine niche. The business found influential people and began to follow them. They too have grown their Twitter following by providing a great customer support. The business has attracted online traffic from U.S and Canada as well as local foot traffic and sales.

Tasti D-Lite: sells frozen yogurt and since its engagement with Twitter, the company has increased sales through creating and offering coupons through Twitter. According to the business management, the coupons issued through the Twitter platform have generated more sales than pay-per-click and targeted ads.

Naked Pizza: sells organic pizza. The business opened its Twitter account at the suggestion of one of its investors. The aim of leveraging Twitter was to cut back on the cost of marketing, create a community around healthy food and eventually improve sales. The company reports that up to

67% of their customers and sales now come from their Twitter community.

Other companies that are successfully using Twitter to drive traffic and sales are Pepsi, American Apparel, Coffe Groundz, Jetblue, Levi's among others.

4

Are You Well Connected In LinkedIn?

LinkedIn has more than 160 million active users, making it the most popular business-networking platform. Linkedin currently adds 10 new members every 5 seconds and the average time on site is about 8 minutes per visit. Linkedin's revenues come from membership subscriptions (20% - only 1% of its members are in premium), advertising (30%) and HR solutions (50%).

As a business, listing your profile on LinkedIn provides you with an opportunity to promote your product/service offering. Listing your business on LinkedIn features you on the Google's search engine, thus providing you with greater visibility. This social networking platform is also a valuable method of finding talented people to hire in your company. Moreover, if you are looking to connect with businesses and key contacts in your field, LinkedIn is where you want to get started.

Setting Up A Linkedin Personal Account

Before setting up your Company Page, I suggest creating a personal profile or optimize the one that you already have.

An optimized profile should have:

1) a picture: by having a photo in your profile you increase by 7 times your chances of having someone clicking through to your profile. Do not upload a logo instead of your own picture as this is against Linkedin's policy.

2) your main keyword/s in six places: headline, current experience, past work experience, summary, specialties and skills & expertise. By doing this, you have a guaranteed higher ranking in the Linkedin search results. A paid profile and a higher number of connections are two other determinant ranking factors.

3) one or more calls to action in the 'Websites' section such as 'Visit My Site' or 'Send Your Question To ...'.

4) additional applications such as: *WordPress* (get your blog posts on Linkedin), *Reading List by Amazon* (current books your are reading or even your own books if you are a published author), *Events* (announce an event you are attending or promote your own event for free), *Polls* (useful for market research), *Box.net* (upload valuable content for your readers to download such as cheat sheets, case studies or reports) and *SlideShare* (share portfolios, video testimonials or slideshows).

WordPress
by WordPress

Connect your virtual lives with the WordPress LinkedIn Application. With the WordPress App, you can sync your WordPress blog posts with your LinkedIn profile, keeping everyone you know in the know.

Reading List by Amazon
by Amazon

Extend your professional profile by sharing the books you're reading with other LinkedIn members. Find out what you should be reading by following updates from your connections, people in your field, or other LinkedIn members of professional interest to you.

Events
by LinkedIn

Find professional events, from conferences to local meet-ups, and make the right connections with other professionals at the event.

Polls
by LinkedIn

The Polls application allows you to collect actionable data from your connections and the professional audience on LinkedIn.

Box.net Files
by Box.net

Add the Box.net Files application to manage all your important files online. Box.net lets you share content on your profile, and collaborate with friends and colleagues.

SlideShare Presentations
by SlideShare Inc

SlideShare is the best way to share presentations on LinkedIn! You can upload & display your own presentations, check out presentations from your colleagues, and find experts within your network.

5) a personalized URL: this can be edited in the 'Public Profile' section. Once claimed, your new URL should be http://linkedin.com/**yourname**

6) recommendations: write recommendations for your connections and ask them to return the favor. When done properly, recommendations can be valuable in enhancing your LinkedIn profile.

When you request a recommendation from someone tell them the aspects that you would like them to focus on while endorsing you or your business. Navigate to the 'Edit profile' section and then click on the 'Request Recommendation' button, to request a recommendation from the LinkedIn platform.

Note that it is not possible to edit these endorsements; you can only request the recommender to edit. If you receive a recommendation that you do not want to make public, use the 'Archive' button to make it private.

7) followers: your main objective as a Linkedin user is to increase the number of people in your network (of 1st, 2nd and 3rd degree), but also to connect with the right audience. You've probably connected already with your friends and customers. So I would like to suggest 3 other ways to increase your followership that are less known:

a) go to the search box and type the word 'LION' which is an abbreviation of 'Linkedin Open Networker'. People that have this term in their headline are accepting every invitation to connect they receive.

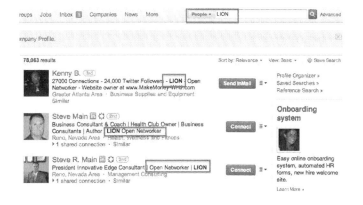

b) **send an invite to connect to people that came to visit your profile**

c) **go to toplinked.com and choose one of the services they offer**

Join Free: you get to download a list of people ('Invite Me List') that are willing to connect with you. You just need to invite them. Note that you are only allowed to invite a maximum of 3,000 people per account.

<u>Monthly Membership</u>: you pay $9.95 per month and you can add yourself to the 'Invite Me List' so people can send you invitation to connect. You'll get an average of 20 to 50 invitations per day. If you are happy to renew your subscription after your first month, I suggest upgrading to an annual membership, which will only cost you $49.95 per year.

Join TopLinked.com:

Account Information

First Name: [   ]

Last Name: [   ]

Email: [   ]

Password: [   ]

Re-type password: [   ]

Select Membership Plan

Add yourself to the Lists: ○ **$9.95/month**

⦿ **$49.95/year** (Best Value - 7 Months FREE!)

List Download Only: ○ **Free** (Invite Me List for LinkedIn Download Only)

[Continue]

8) a list of groups you've joined: as soon as you joined a group in your niche I recommend introducing yourself, posting often relevant articles and comment on other people's posts.

Now that we discussed the Personal Profile, I would like to recommend a great profile to look at which is the one of Lewis Howes, recognized expert in Linkedin: http://www.linkedin.com/in/lewishowes.

Setting Up A Linkedin Company Page

To create your Linkedin Company Page, you need to click on the 'Companies' tab in the menu at the top and then 'Add a Company'. An email address that has your company domain is required and this address will be listed in your business profile. Addresses that are integrated with free services such as Gmail or Yahoo will not work here.

Complete your profile by including:

Administration: LinkedIn requires that you indicate the person who will be administering the business profile. You can include all your employees by offering them a valid email address that is registered to the company domain or nominate specific people.

Logo: you need to upload two logos - a rectangle and a square. The square logo needs to be 50x50 pixels and this logo will accompany all your posts.

Company Description: you have 1500 characters to offer a description of what your business is and what it offers. Include the mission and the vision of your company. Also do not forget to add a call to action. HubSpot's page is the best example in providing a great company description.

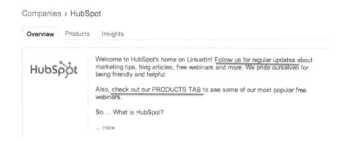

Once you edited your company description, include the specialties. These are basically keywords that your customers will use to find you. See bellow examples of 'specialties' from different companies.

Apple designs Macs, the best personal computers in the world, along with Mac OS X, iLife, iWork, and professional software. Apple leads the digital music revolution with its iPods and iTunes online store. Apple is reinventing the mobile phone with its revolutionary iPhone and App Store, and has recently introduced its magical iPad which is defining the future of mobile media and computing devices.

Specialties
Innovative product development, world class operations, Retail, Telephone Support

LinkedIn takes your professional network online, giving you access to people, jobs and opportunities like never before. Built upon trusted connections and relationships, LinkedIn has established the world's largest and most powerful professional network. Currently, more than 160 million professionals are on LinkedIn, including executives from all five hundred of the Fortune 500 companies, as well as a wide range of household names in technology, financial services, media, consumer packaged goods, entertainment, and numerous other industries. The company is publicly held and has a diversified business model with revenues coming from user subscriptions, advertising sales and hiring solutions.

Specialties
Online Professional Network, Jobs, People Search, Company Search, Address Book, Advertising, Professional Identity, Group Collaboration

Integrating With Twitter And Business Blog RSS Feed: tweets will not longer show on Linkedin (without using a third party tool such as IFTTT – If This Then That) since the beginning of July 2012, however you can still send your LinkedIn status updates to Twitter. More details on this topic is given in the 'Inside the Twitter-LinkedIn divorce' article from Fortune Magazine.

Other Required Details: This section allows you to indicate your company status (operating or out of business), your company size, your company type and the main company industry. You can also insert your website link and include the year when the company was founded.

To feed your blog posts onto your Linkedin Company Page, simply click the RSS tab on your blog to gain access to the newsfeed URL. Copy this URL and then paste it in the Company Blog RSS Feed box. This will allow news and blog posts from your site to appear on your Linkedin Company Page.

Locations: This section describes where your business is located. You may include up to five addresses. Once this is done, select 'Publish' to activate your LinkedIn company profile. Your Page URL should be http://linkedin.com/company/yourcompanyname.

Other Tabs You Could Have On Your Linkedin Company Page: the majority of the companies on Linkedin do not have more than one tab that includes all the information mentioned previously. This tab is called 'Overview'. However I would suggest taking advantage of other tabs that Linkedin has put at your disposal such as *Products & Services, Careers and Insights.*

Companies > LinkedIn

| Overview | Careers | Products & Services | Insights |

Linked in ®   LinkedIn takes your professional network online, giving you access to people, jobs and opportunities like never before. Built upon trusted connections and relationships, LinkedIn has established the world's largest and most powerful professional network. Currently, more than 160 million

... more

In the **Products & Services,** you can list all your products (free and paid) and include product/service recommendations (ask your customers to provide them). You can even link to a sign up page for list building. You can include videos and pictures. See below two examples of Products & Services pages. One is from HubSpot and the other from Linkedin and they are very good examples to learn from.

HubSpot

Learn How to Grow Your Traffic, Leads and Sales with HubSpot

HubSpot is the only all-in-one marketing software platform that helps 6,000+ businesses transform their marketing. **Let's transform your marketing too.**

Schedule a demo and one of HubSpot's experts will:

- Evaluate your website's current performance.
- Identify opportunities to beat your competition online.
- Show you how to convert more visitors into leads.
- Demonstrate how HubSpot tracks the ROI of your marketing efforts.

Fill out the form to the right, and let's get started!

What Do Customers Say?

"I am blown away you what can be done all in one place."
- Cristine Hafner, Hafner Creative

"Since starting with HubSpot, website traffic rose more than double and we 300 visitors per month to over 1,200, and I have already generated a number of leads that pay for HubSpot 10 times over."
- Noel Huelsenbeck, Vocio

"HubSpot is without the one place to easily change our perspective and focus & right when we want to be quickly. I couldn't be more important."
- Todd Hammill, Wired2Fish

Get a Custom Demonstration of HubSpot

First Name *

Last Name *

Company Name *

Company Email (please no personal) *

Phone *

Website *

Role at company *
- Please Select -

Number of Employees *
- Please Select -

My Business Primarily Sells to Other Businesses (B2B) or Consumers (B2C) *
- Please Select -

My company provides marketing services such as PR, SEO, Web Design or other e-Marketing *
- Please Select -

When are you available for a demonstration? *

See HubSpot in Action

Companies > LinkedIn

carousel presentation

Finding Online Communities That Align With Your Professional Interests

LinkedIn Groups are a great way of finding and connecting with people in your niche and with whom you share interests. These groups allow you to:

a) Easily find popular discussions in your professional networks.

b) Participate in these discussions by commenting, liking and sharing.

c) Follow key contacts in your groups by using the 'Top Influencers tool' (found on the right of your group page) or by simply reviewing their profile to view their group activity.

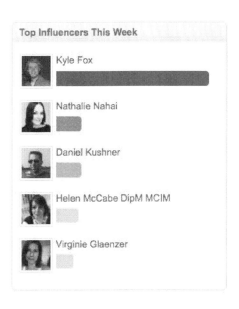

d) Contribute by posting relevant and useful content such as: posts, links to articles and upcoming events, infographics, videos, statistics, discounts, etc. You can also recommend products, ask for opinions or create free polls within the group (if option enabled). The content you post could be yours or curated.

e) Directly message each member of a group.

Would you please link with a fellow Global Open Networker with 7850+ Connections ?

 David Taylor · Utility Warehouse Distributor in London and Professional Genealogical Researcher - 4th Most Connected on Linked In

Email received from a group member

You and David Taylor share a network or group.

Hi Adina

TOGETHER WE ARE STRONG - TOGETHER WE WILL GROW

I joined Linkedin on 30th December as part of my New Years resolution to reach out across the world and contact as many people as I could to learn and to pass on any knowledge I may have.

I have become a dedicated LION Open Networker based in London and have come into contact with some wonderful people who have helped and encouraged me to build my network to 7850 contacts in 5 1/2 months.

I would like to meet and contact even more people, but I have now run out of invites and I would welcome invites from my fellow LION's who wish to spread the Good News of Open Networking.

My e-mail is avidt@yahoo.co.uk

Many Thanks .

David Taylor

It is advisable that you join just a few groups that reflect your business/professional interests. In this way, you can add as many people, as you want in your network.

To get started joining a group:

Go to the navigation bar and scan through the 'Groups' link. Then, select the 'Groups' directory link from the drop-down menu; this will take you to the 'Groups Directory' page.

Describe the type of group that you are looking to join using relevant keywords. For instance, if you are looking to join a group focused on 'Internet marketing' simply type in 'internet marketing' in the search box. Next, click on the search button to view a list of groups that relate to your keywords. Click the group owner's name if you want more details about this group. Send the owner a message requesting for some information about the group.

When you find a group to join simply click on the 'Join Group' tab on the right side of the group profile. You will be directed to the Group's full profile and information such as how you will communicate with the group. You may also choose to have the group profile appear on your profile once you join.

You will receive a message confirming your application. Some groups allow you to join automatically after approval while others refer you to the group administrator who will manually approve you. Remember to introduce (who you are, what you are looking for and how you can help) once part of the group.

Answering Questions To Show Expertise And Gain Trust

The 'Answers' feature on LinkedIn allows you to ask and answer questions asked by other LinkedIn users. This feature is located at the top of the screen, under the 'More' menu. There are more than 2 million answers so far.

You can choose to answer questions in a wide array of categories, depending on your expertise. There are 22 business categories to choose from including career, government, non-profit and health. Answering questions in your niche showcases your expertise, enhances your trust with potential customers and makes you the go-to person for solutions in your niche. It also allows you to meet new people and to expand your network.

<u>To get started</u>:

Select categories that you are an expert in and can provide relevant answers.

Look through these categories to see the type of questions that other users are asking. Choose to answer questions that add value to the person who asked and other users as well.

Before answering the questions, look through the details. If the question already features some comments, you can still include your own opinion or comment on the comments.

Before publishing answers make sure that you proofread them to avoid mistakes that could hurt your credibility and expertise. Once the Question is closed to further Answers, your Answer may be voted as the 'Best Answer' by the person that asked the Question.

Dedicate some of your networking time to answering questions and you will be surprised at how this can expand your network and generate warm prospect with whom you can do business. Include with each answer a personalized signature including links to whichever page you'd like to drive traffic.

Linkedin Advertising Program

The LinkedIn advertising platform offers an excellent opportunity to generate leads. Being primarily a business-networking platform, the advertising messages that you air-on this platform are more likely to be well received by warm prospects.

AdWords target people based on what they are looking for. So you should use Adwords for promoting consumer products, where consumers are at different levels in the buying cycle. **Facebook ads** target people based on who they are and their interests. So you should use Facebook advertising if you want to increase brand awareness and fan engagement. **Twitter ads** target people based on what they talk about and who they follow. **Linkedin ads** target both individuals and businesses based on what they do and the industry they are in.

Who's on LinkedIn

Members	Who You Can Target	
160M World Wide	**7.9M** Business Decision Makers	**1.3M** Small Business Owners
40M U.S. Based	**5.5M** High Tech Managers	**4.2M** Corporate Executives

LinkedIn ads feature an image, a headline with just 24 characters, and a description with 75 characters. The advertisements that you pay for will appear in one or two places within the LinkedIn interface. The first section is on the sidebar or at the bottom of the page; these ads can include text and an image. If you choose to have a text only ad, it will appear at the top of the interface. See examples below of side ads, bottom ads and text top ad.

You may pay for the ads on a cost-per-click (CPC) or cost per impression basis (CPM). To make the most of the LinkedIn advertising platform, create ads that will effectively communicate your message. The LinkedIn ads are typically short, thus each character is important. LinkedIn enables you to direct other users to your business website or to a products and services page on your LinkedIn company pages.

In addition to promoting your products and services, you may also promote groups and company pages. Make use of the new feature that allows you to post status updates to your company pages. To make your ads more effective, refine your target audience by job title, industry or groups.

Look at 'LinkedIn Today' to keep abreast with the trending news in various industries and to gain insights about your audience. When you know the type of news your audience is sharing, you will understand the types of offers that may trigger their interests.

It is recommended that you create three variations of your ad campaigns including varying title, images and calls to action. These ads will be displayed only to the audience that you have selected. The ad with the highest click-through-rates will be displayed frequently and will attract additional clicks. It is possible to adjust your settings so that all your ads get an equal number of impressions. Be sure to get rid of ads that have low click through rates and monitor those that are successful.

On LinkedIn, the amount that you want to spend on a daily basis is your budget. Ads appear at varying rates throughout the day depending on the users' level of activity. Half of your ad budget is likely to be used up in the morning with the other quarters divided between the afternoon and night. Your ad will not show when your daily budget reaches its limit. An ad budget that is too low may impact negatively on the impressions your ads receive. To determine that your daily budget is adequate, compute the amount that you spent each day in the last week and compare it to your daily budget. Increase your daily budget if these amounts are close or equal to each other.

Whenever a prospect visits your LinkedIn pages, a bidding process transpires between you and fellow advertisers. LinkedIn offers you the range in which other advertisers are bidding. If your bid is high enough, it is likely to win the bidding process. If you overlook the suggested bid range, your bid will have fewer chances of winning the auction. This will result to limited clicks/ impressions.

Finally, you want to measure the effectiveness of your ads. Track the click through rate; **LinkedIn views ads with a CTR of more than 0.0025 as performing well.** It is a good idea to frequently measure your CTRs to track any declines that may require you to create a new ad or tweak the existing one. Narrowing your audience strategically can boost the CTR.

It is also important to measure the leads that your ads are generating. This is particularly helpful if you use ads to direct users to your website. While a high CTR is impressive, neglecting the landing page on your site might lower the conversion rate of visitor to warm prospects.

Other than display ads in LinkedIn you can also send 'Partner Messages' or create 'Polls'.

Sending Partner Messages

You get to create a custom mail (see example below) and LinkedIn will send it on your behalf to your chosen audience. You'll be paying by recipient and the typical open rates are 12%-25%.

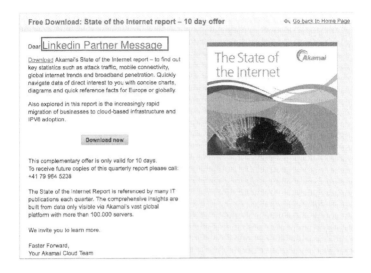

Creating Polls

This feature is located at the top of the screen, under the 'More' menu. You are allowed to create up to 10 polls at the time and for each poll you can have a question (of 120 characters) and up to 5 answers (0f 40 characters each). You can also 'Rotate the order of your answers' if you want.

Your poll has been created ×

Increase participation by sharing your poll on Twitter or Facebook, or by embedding it in your website.

| Tweet | Share | Embed | http://linkd.in/LGAXJW |

Vote on your new poll below, or leave a comment on the results page.

Once you created your poll, you can tweet it, share it on Facebook, embed it on your blog or copy the URL and post it in the discussion forum of your group. You can also promote your poll to the entire LinkedIn network where you'll be paying per response. See below an example of a poll organized by Skype.

LinkedIn Polls

Does working from home really work?
○ Yes. I'm living proof.
○ It's great every once in a while.
○ For some. But not for me.
○ No. Work is for the office.

Vote
or see results

Sponsored By
skype

The results of the poll and the comments are made visible to all LinkedIn users.

Does working from home really work?

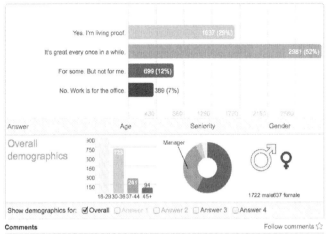

Organizing Webinars By Utilizing The Events Section

Linkedin is a valuable tool for organizing, hosting and promoting events, whether offline or online. The events application on LinkedIn allows you to announce a webinar to people in your niche and to engage with the community before and after the event.

To get started, simply download the Event Application from the applications directory. Click the 'More' tab to gain access to the applications directory.

After adding the event or webinar, LinkedIn will promote it automatically across the network to reach the first-degree connections you have on the platform. As such, when a connection indicates that they are attending your webinar, those in his own network will also be updated about this event. This enables even those in your second and third degree connection to attend the webinar. You can also inform your group members about it or promote it on your company page in the 'status updates'.

When entering your event details, note that you are allowed to upload an image and add a link to an offsite registration page to collect attendee's details.

Digital Accelerator - 3 Day Training Course
July 16, 2012 at 9:00 AM - July 18, 2012 at 5:00 PM
Wallacespace, Covent Garden, London

This event requires registration: http://www.emarketeers.com/training-courses/digital-accelerator

Digital Marketing continues to evolve at such as rapid pace, it has become critical to gain a clear understanding of the key online marketing disciplines. This 3 day training course held in London is led by a team of highly experienced Internet and digital marketers. It will provide delegates with...

Show more...

I'm Attending   Follow

In addition to the automatic promotion that you receive from LinkedIn, you should also consider the LinkedIn advertising program by buying targeted cost per click or cost per impression ads.

To search for events in your industry, just go to http://events.linkedin.com/.

Linked in ®

Home   What is LinkedIn?   Join Today   Sign In

Events Directory

Browse by industry

Accounting Events	Law Practice Events
Airlines/Aviation Events	Legal Services Events
Alternative Dispute Resolution Events	Leisure, Travel & Tourism Events
Alternative Medicine Events	Libraries Events
Animation Events	Logistics And Supply Chain Events
Apparel & Fashion Events	Luxury Goods & Jewelry Events
Architecture & Planning Events	Machinery Events
Arts And Crafts Events	Management Consulting Events
Automotive Events	Maritime Events
Aviation & Aerospace Events	Market Research Events
Banking Events	Marketing And Advertising Events
Biotechnology Events	Mechanical Or Industrial Engineering Events
Broadcast Media Events	Media Production Events
Building Materials Events	Medical Devices Events
Business Supplies And Equipment Events	Medical Practice Events
Capital Markets Events	Mental Health Care Events

Examples Of Businesses That Drive Traffic And Sales With Their LinkedIn Account

New Home Star: is a business-to-business company that offers sales services for homebuilders. The employees at the company use LinkedIn with their own profiles to find prospects and to connect with them. According to the company founder David Rice, the business has expanded to serve a dozen markets in just less than three years.

Hewlett-Packard: there are more than 684,792 Hewlett-Packard followers on LinkedIn. The company's product and service pages on LinkedIn have more than 3,200 recommendations for the 19 products and services that it offers.

For the company, this has translated to 'word of mouth' marketing for its products, which has boosted sales significantly. According to Hewlett-Packard, a good approach is to display your products and services on your company pages and then ask satisfied customers to offer recommendations.

5

What Did You StumbleUpon Today?

StumbleUpon, with 25 million users, is a social tool that enables users to find interesting web pages and recommend them to their social network contacts. The site allows people with the same interests to connect, bookmark and share the content they find online. As a business, StumbleUpon enables you to find people in your niche. When you find these people, you can begin to engage them by sharing diverse and relevant content. As a social media tool, StumbleUpon enables you to expand your connections and boost traffic - isn't that what you are in business for? Here is how a business can leverage StumbleUpon.

Setting Up StumbleUpon For Business

To get started with StumbleUpon, you need to sign up for an account. Visit the homepage at http://www.stumbleupon.com and then click on the yellow tab that invites you to join the network.

You may login through your Facebook account by clicking on the 'Login In With Facebook' link. A username and password will automatically be created. You may also log in by filling out the application form. Submit the registration form by clicking on the 'Sign Up' tab.

Next, include your topics of interest; choose at least 5. Preferably, these should be topics related to your business niche. However, make your range of topics of interest wide enough to attract even more users with whom you might share interests. Adding favorite topics to your profile will show other users the items that interest you and that you are an active member. They will be more compelled to follow you. Here are my selected topics:

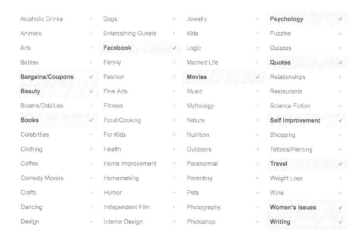

Alcoholic Drinks	Dogs	Jewelry	**Psychology** ✓
Animals	Entertaining Guests	Kids	Puzzles
Arts	**Facebook** ✓	Logic	Quizzes
Babies	Family	Married Life	**Quotes** ✓
Bargains/Coupons ✓	Fashion	**Movies** ✓	Relationships
Beauty ✓	Fine Arts	Music	Restaurants
Bizarre/Oddities	Fitness	Mythology	Science Fiction
Books ✓	Food/Cooking	Nature	**Self Improvement** ✓
Celebrities	For Kids	Nutrition	Shopping
Clothing	Health	Outdoors	Tattoos/Piercing
Coffee	Home Improvement	Paranormal	**Travel** ✓
Comedy Movies	Homemaking	Parenting	Weight Loss
Crafts	Humor	Pets	Wine
Dancing	Independent Film	Photography	**Women's Issues** ✓
Design	Interior Design	Photoshop	**Writing** ✓

Once you selected your chosen topics (additional interests can be added at anytime by clicking on the 'Discover' tab), StumbleUpon will provide you with a short 'how to guide' on how to use their toolbar, sitting just under your browser bar.

Use the StumbleBar to explore your interests with StumbleUpon:
You'll see the StumbleBar on the top of every web page as you Stumble.

Every time you click the "Stumble!" button, we'll show you something new based on your interests.

Like or Dislike web pages to improve the quality of our recommendations for you.

Type a short word or phrase (e.g. 'chili recipes') and Stumble through related web pages.

Stumble through a specific interest or Channel you're following.

Share content you like with connections including friends, family and your social networks.

Browse your Likes, adjust your settings and explore more.

And now you are ready to start stumbling by clicking on the 'Stumble!' tab at the top left. Every time you click on this tab, StumbleUpon will show you a different web page based on your interests. You can also add new pages you find interesting on the web. To vote on a page, you either click on the 'thumbs up' if you like it or 'thumbs down' if you dislike it. By doing this, you will not only personalize your own experience, but also the experience of other users.

Next I suggest installing the StumbleUpon tool bar from http://stumbleupon.com/downloads as this will allow you to add to StumbleUpon new pages you found interesting on the web.

To customize your profile, go to the 'Settings' menu. Remember to include links to your social profiles (Facebook, Twitter, LinkedIn and Google), website and blogs. These are 'no follow' links but they will help you attract traffic when other users visit your profile and are interested in what you 'Stumble'. Include a description and a picture, to make your profile complete and approachable. Customize your URL to http://stumbleupon.com/stumbler/**yourusername**. Note that your username can only be changed once so think carefully when you set it up.

Other than creating a profile, you can also **set up your own StumbleUpon channel**. There are three types of StumbleUpon channels: *Site Channels* (with the latest news in technology and interesting videos sites), *Person Channels* (with celebrity news) and *Brand Channels* (with commercials and deals from well known brands). Channels can be followed and un-followed if you change your mind. And content can be liked (thumbs up) and disliked (thumbs down). If a page got lots of dislikes, StumbleUpon will remove it.

Site Channels

Site Channels ⬍

1x.com - Sublime Photo
Site Channel
1,129 Pages | 11K Followers
⊞FOLLOW

500px
Site Channel
436 Pages | 15K Followers
⊞FOLLOW

7x7SF
Site Channel
1,716 Pages | 5,089 Followers
⊞FOLLOW

8tracks
Site Channel
968 Pages | 20K Followers
⊞FOLLOW

ABC News
Site Channel
2,643 Pages | 7,928 Followers
⊞FOLLOW

Adweek
Site Channel
2,054 Pages | 6,537 Followers
⊞FOLLOW

Allrecipes.com
Site Channel
249 Pages | 667 Followers
⊞FOLLOW

Architectural Digest
Site Channel
184 Pages | 9,018 Followers
⊞FOLLOW

Person Channels

Person Channels ⬍

Ashley Benson
Person Channel
289 Pages | 6,339 Followers
⊞FOLLOW

Ashley Tisdale
Person Channel
189 Pages | 1,964 Followers
⊞FOLLOW

Ben Folds
Person Channel
231 Pages | 2,357 Followers
⊞FOLLOW

Billy Joel
Person Channel
95 Pages | 2,900 Followers
⊞FOLLOW

Chelsea Handler
Person Channel
168 Pages | 7,387 Followers
⊞FOLLOW

CultsCultsCults
Person Channel
42 Pages | 2,024 Followers
⊞FOLLOW

Emmitt Smith
Person Channel
2 Pages | 142 Followers
⊞FOLLOW

Enrique Iglesias
Person Channel
141 Pages | 3,030 Followers
⊞FOLLOW

Brand Channels

Brand Channels ⬍

(RED)
Brand Channel
79 Pages | 6,527 Followers
⊞FOLLOW

2 Broke Girls
Brand Channel
228 Pages | 7,753 Followers
⊞FOLLOW

A&E
Brand Channel
18K Pages | 10K Followers
⊞FOLLOW

Adult Swim
Brand Channel
76 Pages | 50K Followers
⊞FOLLOW

Animal Planet
Brand Channel
801 Pages | 13K Followers
⊞FOLLOW

Around The Horn
Brand Channel
402 Pages | 5,920 Followers
⊞FOLLOW

Astralwerks
Brand Channel
90 Pages | 4,752 Followers
⊞FOLLOW

Audi
Brand Channel
171 Pages | 8,205 Followers
⊞FOLLOW

If you want your blog content to become a channel on StumbleUpon, you need to send an email to <partners@stumbleupon.com>. Having a channel on StumbleUpon is a great opportunity for brand awareness, market research (you'll see what kind of content they like the most) and increase in traffic. The more followers you have, the more of your content will be seen.

Connecting With StumbleUpon Users

Every time you visit the profile of another user on StumbleUpon, you will see their image and statistics that tell you their level of activity on the platform. You will also see the interests you share with the user, based on both your favorite items and those that you have given a thumbs up.

Following A Stumbler: This is a good first step in building connections and eventually an interactive relationship with Stumblers. When you choose to follow a user (**you can follow a maximum of 500 members**), you have the option to allow their shares to your StumbleUpon toolbar. This means that when the person you are following shares something with you, this item will be displayed in 'share' pannel. Also all their 'likes' will show in your 'recommended' pages.

Once you begin following someone, you will want them to return the favor. Do this by sending a message telling them that you are a follower of theirs and would like them to follow you back, so you can exchange interesting content. You also have the option of reviewing their posts and then sending a message informing them that you have reviewed their post, and ask them to follow you back.

Sharing: You will receive many shares, but only give a thumb up for the posts that you like. Further, engage with your following by reviewing an item. This will go a long way in attracting others to offer feedback to your own items as well. Providing feedback will help you strengthen the relationship you have with other users.

As you build your following, use the toolbar to share items.

Accompany the items you share with a brief message telling your recipient why you are sharing the item. Note that StumbleUpon does not allow you to send shares to all your followers. It is also important that you do not share too many items with your followers, as this will cause them to un-follow you or block shares from you by clicking on the 'stop shares from this user'. Share moderately but stay active; a post per day is sufficient. Share information that is relevant and that will interest your followers.

Thumbing Up A Post: The 'Thumb Up' feature is valuable especially for every business that looks to boost traffic to their website. This feature is similar to the 'Like' feature on Facebook.   When you click the 'Thumb Up', you are essentially engaging with other users and in particular the originator of that post.

It is possible to Thumb a post that has already been thumbed up by other users on the network. If you are the first one to 'Thumb Up' a post you found across the web, you will be prompted to review the post as a new discovery. Offering feedback to other people's posts is a great way to start building a relationship with them. Be sure to include a title, description and tags to the posts that you discover and review.

Add a New Page

Web page address	
Is this page safe for work?	○Yes ○No, it contains nudity or adult content
What's this page about?	Select an Interest ⌄
Add Tags (optional)	
	Enter tags separated by commas
Write a comment (optional)	
What's the page's language?	English ⌄
	Add This Page

In addition to Thumbing Up and sharing other users' posts, you too can add and share your own content. Once you add your posts to the network, they will appear on the comprehensive StumbleUpon directory, allowing other users to come across it. It is possible to 'Thumb Up' your own content, but the essence of StumbleUpon is to have other users engage with your content and recommend it to others. A good approach to take is to 'Thumb Up' only one out of every item of yours. Alternatively, use the 'Share' option on the toolbar to suggest your posts to your followers, with the anticipation that they will read, find it interesting and then Thumb it Up.

Making Your Content More Visible

Here are some of the ways you can make your content more visible to other Stumblers:

Customize Your Page: Complete your profile (as well as your interests) to allow people to know who you are. Include your brand logo or your image as the avatar and share your interests and detailed biography.

Stumble Frequently: StumbleUpon is a social media network and your own level of activity will determine how other users will engage with you. It is not enough to just stumble upon and submit one page. Other users will view you as inactive and will be reluctant to interact with you. On the contrary, frequent stumbles and submissions will make you more visible and a highly ranked member of the community.

Optimize Your Submitted Content: Make your page tags relevant as you submit your content. Relevant tags allow you to generate targeted traffic from Stumblers who are interested in the tagged topic. Use keywords and tags wisely to avoid lowering your community rating by stuffing keywords in your page labels. It is possible for other users to add or remove the tags you include in the submissions.

Pay To Have Your Links Showed To Stumblers: Paid Discovery is the advertising model of StumbleUpon where you pay to show your content. Only 5% of the stumbles are reserved for advertising and you can pay between $0.05 to $0.25 if you plan to target the 'most engaged users'. When a paid stumble is shown to you, you'll see the 'sponsored' tab showing in the toolbar.

StumbleUpon For Brand Marketing

As seen above, StumbleUpon has great potential to attract traffic to your site. This further opens another opportunity to market your brand and to make it more visible to specific people interested in your niche. Additionally, you can use this tool in your content marketing campaign, especially when you are looking for new content to write about. Here are a few tips for business brand marketing:

Share Strategically: Keep in mind that StumbleUpon is a sharing community whose users are looking for diverse content. Share relevant content that will compel your followers to take action. Also, share more than just your own pages. Include an RSS feed in your content to offer your audience more content on a regular basis. Casual readers might become loyal, giving you an opportunity to build a relationship.

Make Your URL Memorable: Use the StumbleUpon URL shortener to create an easy to remember URL that you can share with your followers on the platform. The URL shortener also allows you to track the performance of the stumbles you submit. Use Su.pr link shortener to see the number of retweets as well as clicks your submissions have received. This tool also enables you to see the source of traffic for the pages you share.

Participate: The best way to garner a strong following on a social community is to get involved. Leverage the power of StumbleUpon by making friends (who might become warm prospects for your business) through content sharing, offering feedback, sharing interesting posts and keeping your business profile up to date.

Stumble the Right Stuff: When linking, make sure to link to a page with targeted information. If you are marketing one of your products or cross promoting another business, link to the product page and not to the homepage. This will lower your bounce rate, as people should not have to dig for the product information. In other words, make your content easily accessible.

Do not Sell, Interest: Hard selling does not work well in social communities, including StumbleUpon. While people do not like being sold to, they will not mind seeing what you have to offer. As such, point Stumblers to interesting sites, valuable pages and information that will help them make better purchasing decisions. Use a conversational tone to point users to your product offering. Instead of asking them to buy, tell them the benefits of using your product instead. Interested users will come to your site to make a purchase.

Do Not Automate: To get the most from StumbleUpon, you need to actively and genuinely engage your audience. This is the best way to find out their true needs and to create ways of meeting these needs. Thus, avoid using any tools that will automate your responses or promise to drive traffic to your site from StumbleUpon. In addition to being inauthentic and unhelpful for your marketing campaign, StumbleUpon has banned these tools.

6

Building Your Business Image Through Flickr

Businesses that are high on visuals can leverage the power of images to market their businesses and to interact with their customers. These businesses include those in niches such as photography and design, restaurants and travel, galleries, advertising corporations as well as fashion shops. Flickr, with more than 50 million users, is an online social community that hosts images and videos posted by people from all over the world. There are more than 7 billion images already uploaded.

Businesses are using this platform to enhance their brands online and to improve their visibility at the search engines. When you upload photos on Flickr, search engines index them. This can help enhance your visibility as well as generate traffic to your business website. Additionally, Flickr is a social community in which you can interact with other users by commenting on their images and sharing the images across other social networks.

Setting Up Flickr For Business

Signing Up: To make the most of Flickr, start by creating a free and basic account. Visit the site homepage at http://www.flickr.com, and then click on 'Create Your Account.' You need a Yahoo account to sign up with Flickr. If you do not yet have one, simply click on the 'Sign Up' link to create a yahoo account.

If you already have a Yahoo ID, simply login with your username and password. Flickr will take you through a step-by-step process in which you will choose your screen name. The screen name can be the same or different from your username. You will also need to choose an icon and edit your profile. You may edit your profile as many times as you need to; to do this, simply click on your username at the top right side of the interface.

Adding Photos To Your Flickr Account: Photos are the lifeline of Flickr. You can include any photo as long as it is appropriate. Also, ensure that you do not infringe on copyright laws by using copyrighted images. Check to see that the images you use are under Creative Commons License; such images are free to use as long as you include an attribute to the image owner or the source. It is also a good idea to allow others to use your original photos under the

Creative Commons License. Those who use your images on Flickr will give you credit in the form of your name and a link to your Flickr URL.

To upload images on Flickr, click on the arrow close to 'You" and then scroll down to find the link 'Upload Photos and Videos.' Click on this link and then on 'Choose Photos and Videos' option; this will direct you to where you have stored the images to be uploaded. Then, click 'Enter' upon choosing the photos that you want to upload. You are limited to 300MB of photos each month.

Next, select your privacy settings. As a business, it is advisable that you keep your settings public so that anyone can view your images. Click 'Upload Photos and Videos' to upload all the images. You will then be prompted to add a description to your photos after the uploading process is complete. Briefly describe your photos using the relevant, business specific keywords to optimize the photos. Also, add tags in the tags area, location and company name to make the images visible.

Use the 'Add to a Set' option to sort your images into small sets, especially if you have uploaded bulk images. Sets simply make it easy for other users to find specific images.

For example if you are a boutique fashion store, you might want to divide your photos into sets such as 'shoes', 'kids' boots', 'women's clothing' etc.

Optimize the images further by including keyword rich titles. In the description area, describe your business, your product and tell users why they want to purchase your product/ service. Remember to link to the appropriate pages in your website. For example if you upload a picture of kids' coats, link this to the product page for kids' items instead of the website homepage. Invest your time to optimize each image in this way.

To add a picture to another social network, such as Twitter you may have to do this manually. Click on the 'Share' link on each image, on 'Blog It' and then the link to the social networking site to which you are sharing the image. Always accompany your shared images with a description that will show the recipient why you sent them the image.

To delete or edit the information on a photo or the photo itself, simply click on the photo's description. This will take you to the 'Actions' menu, which will offer you a list of options including delete and edit.

Managing Your Contacts

As you upload photos on Flickr daily, your contacts will receive email notifications from Flickr about the content you have uploaded. This will prompt your contacts to check out your newly uploaded images or to buy one of your displayed products. Your contacts will receive these notifications only if you upload content regularly. So take the time to post at least one photo each week. This is an excellent way to stay in touch and visible to your customers.

To find your contacts, navigate to the arrow net to 'Contacts' on your Flickr homepage. Use the 'Find Your Friends' suggested option and apply the email option that you prefer. This allows Flickr to crawl your email to find contacts that are already on Flickr. Then, add your email contacts to your Flickr contact list so that they can receive notifications when you upload new content. This approach is especially helpful when you are just getting started on the platform.

Use the search option to find people who might be interested in your image stream and then include them in your contact list. This is a great way to find people who might be interested in your product/service offering. Even though you might not start to sell to them directly, finding them is a good first step. For example as a boutique fashion shop, search for other Flickr users who often upload fashion related images. Simply add them in your contact and if they accept, they will become your 'friends' on Flickr.

Joining Flickr Groups

Flickr groups offer you the opportunity to engage with your clients, meet potential customers as well key contacts in your niche. Additionally, more people will view your images.

To join a group, first search for a group or groups in your niche or related niches. Look for groups that your target audience is likely to participate in. Enter a relevant search term related to your niche for example 'real estate' and then see what this brings. Groups have their own regulations for membership and most place a limit on the number of photos you can upload to the group space each month. These groups are social, interactive communities; it is essential that you participate actively by providing relevant comments, holding discussions and frequently posting. By offering others your feedback, they too will engage with you in the same way, thereby building a relationship.

After finding a suitable group, click on 'Join This Group,' an option located just below the group name. You need to upload photos to your Flickr account before sharing them with the group. Additionally, you need to upload at least five photos on your account before other people in your group can see the images.

Next, go to the images that you want to make visible to the group. Ensure that the images you upload have the relevant keywords or tags and that the images are Public. Click on the 'Actions' link above the photo and then choose the option 'Add to a Group.' Use the dropdown menu to select the appropriate group.

Groups, like sets, will allow you to collate images under a specific theme in which other group users upload their images too. This makes finding images much easier. Use the forum platform to participate in group discussions.

Sharing Your Flickr Photos

Being a social community, Flickr allows you and other users to share images with your connections, on other social networks. You can share images through several options including:

a) Through your blog, Twitter and Facebook by linking Flickr to these platforms

b) Creating a Flickr web address and then sharing it with friends, clients and potential customers, for example: http://www.flickr.com/photos/yourusername/

c) Sharing images via email or embedding your image link using HTML snippets. Use the share menu at the top of a photo to share in this way

d) Sending your Flickr links to your audience

e) Adding a Flickr button to your website

Sharing Your Flickr Videos

Although Flickr is primarily a photo-sharing platform, users can also post videos. If you sign up for a Pro (paid and only $1.87/month) account, you can upload videos that other users can watch in high definition format.

Recently, Flickr made it possible for users with a free account to post two videos each month. Members with a paid account can upload an unlimited number of videos at 90 seconds max and 500MB per video. Admittedly, with only 90 seconds, Flickr videos are short but they can make an interesting addition to your photo collection. You can use the short videos to subtly promote a product or to simply entertain your audience.

With Pro you get:

- **Unlimited** photo uploads (50MB per photo)
- **Unlimited** video uploads (90 seconds max, 500MB per video)
- The ability to show HD **Video**
- **Unlimited** storage
- **Unlimited** bandwidth
- **Archiving** of high-resolution original images
- The ability to **replace a photo**
- Post any of your photos or videos in **up to 60 group pools**
- View count and referrer **statistics**
- Limitation of maximum **image size available** to others
- **Ad-free** browsing and sharing

Compare that to what you get with a Free Account:

- **300 MB** monthly photo upload limit (30MB per photo)
- **2** video uploads each month (90 seconds max, 150MB per video)
- Photostream views limited to the **200 most recent images**
- Post any of your photos in **up to 10 group pools**
- Only **smaller (resized) images** accessible (though the originals are saved in case you upgrade later)

Marketing Your Business With Flickr

Online users are more attracted by compelling images than they are by textual content. With a rapidly growing community, Flickr offers a timely opportunity to use targeted and optimized images to market your products/services and to make your brand more visible. It is possible to drive traffic and sales by using this platform for your marketing strategy.

However, bear in mind that Flickr is a photo-sharing site and outright commercial activities such as promoting and advertising your products and services are prohibited. As such, you must be creative in how you market your products.

<u>Here are some Flickr marketing strategies for your business</u>:

Make Your Website URL Your Flickr Screen Name: Your Flickr screen name will accompany most of the activities that you undertake including the images you upload as well as the comments you post in Group forums. Using your web URL as your screen name, markets your business site. You can further mention your business and website in the image descriptions and tag areas.

Advertise Your Brand And Products On Your Profile: As you create your Flickr profile, vividly describe your brand as well as your product/service offering. Tell other users what your business is all about but make this less of a sales pitch and more informational. Upload the 'Buddy' button and use your brand logo as your Flickr icon.

Upload Relevant Photos: Photos should give a true picture of your business and what it offers. However, do not limit the images you upload to your business only, source for and use other images that are related to your niche. Describe your photos and optimize them for the search engines but avoid outright selling.

Participate In The Community: Participation allows you to engage directly with other users while telling them about your brand and products. Add photos that interest you, to your 'Favorites' list and share these images with Flickr users or your connections on popular social networks such as Facebook, Pinterest, Google+ and Twitter. When joining groups, join those associated with your location including your state, city or neighborhood; this is an excellent way to connect with local customers and prospects.

Link Your Website To Your Image Stream On Flickr: This allows site visitors to easily view your photo gallery on Flickr. If the site visitors are Flickr users already, they might include you in their contact list. By linking your website to Flickr, your website already has a free link making it even more prominent in major search engines including Google and Yahoo.

7

Getting Started On Viadeo

Viadeo, with more than 45 million worldwide users, is the second largest social networking platform after LinkedIn targeting businesses and professionals. As a business, Viadeo enables you to meet key contacts in your niche, engage in niche specific discussions and identify opportunities to expand your business. Through this platform, you can also identify ideal candidates and recruit them to your team, with minimal costs involved.

Setting Up Viadeo For Business

To get started on Viadeo, you need to create your business profile. A complete profile will not only improve your visibility but will also expose you to more business opportunities. Make your profile friendly and trustworthy by adding your photo. Profiles that feature a picture attract more visits than profiles that do not have a photo.

Remember to optimize your profile for the search results on related topics. Use keywords related to your brand and niche industry in both the profile title and the description area.

Finding Contacts You Know

After completing your profile, it is time to find people to connect with. Some of your contacts may already be active members on the platform. Viadeo will import your email contacts and add these people into your contact list.

You may also use Viadeo's search box to find people by their last name, company or school if they are not in your email contact list. Another approach to finding valuable connections is to use second-degree connections to grow your contact base on this platform. These connections are also known as the 'contacts of your contacts.' Invite the people in your third degree connection to join your network.

Share your business cards across the platform. Other contacts will also be inclined to share their contact details with you. Additionally, you will be notified automatically when any of your contacts updates their contact information. You can share both your business and personal contact cards depending on the nature of interaction you might have with another member.

In addition to finding contacts and adding them to your network, it is a good idea to actively engage with them. This is especially important if you connect with a key contact that might be valuable to your business. Set your news feed to send you updates on the activities the people you are following are engaged in. Also, comment and offer feedback when the members you are following post content on the network. Show your expertise in a certain niche by posting your own content; make it professional and highly engaging for your business/professional readers.

Use tags to organize your contacts. This will enable you to easily find your connections as your list grows. Tagging also helps you to remember how and when you met, notifies you about your 'to do list' and activities to carry out in relation to your contacts, for example attend a small business-networking event that one of your contacts has invited you to.

Viadeo Groups

Video Groups provide an excellent environment for meeting local business owners, key industry contacts, industry professionals as well as ideal candidates. These groups essentially offer a platform for you to make your business more visible, to closely locate relevant opportunities and to better engage with those in your network. If you are looking for business-to-business opportunities and collaborations, invest your time in the professional Groups.

Viadeo allows you to participate in different Groups that appeal to your business niche and interests. Before joining a Group, you can preview it to see if it offers what you are looking for. Each Group on Viadeo offers a common wall or bulletin board for opportunities and pertinent announcements, a list of niche-relevant events, and a discussion forum where members share advice and users generated news.

Targeted Advertising

Viadeo offers a rich localization platform given that its services are offered in English, Dutch, Italian, French, Portuguese and Spanish. This allows you to target your content as well as your advertisement campaign to a very specific audience on the platform. While the targeted advertising on Viadeo can be quite costly for a small business, there are significant benefits that come with leveraging the program. These include:

a) Connecting and engaging with your targeted audience irrespective of their language. Your target audience is likely to include complementary businesses or professionals looking for work.

b) Making your brand more visible to prospective customers.

c) Meeting your advertising objectives and measuring the return on investment of your ad campaign.

Viadeo lets you target your ad camping based on the profiles of members on the platform. You can target members based on:

a) Their profile title, niche industry, geo-localization and their professional position

b) Their educational background, business background, websites and blogs

c) Their Group membership and keywords

Recruiting Your Team

Millions of users on Viadeo are looking to make professional connections and to find work that matches their skill sets. As a small business, you know how difficult it can be finding qualified people who understand the essence of your business. Additionally advertising, sourcing and recruiting can be costly and takes up so much time.

Viadeo allows you to easily discover ideal and talented candidates from a pool of more than 45 million members. It offers an environment that enables you to build formidable relationships with contacts who can point you to candidates that will understand your business.

As you source for candidates to recruit to your team, take into consideration the return on investment. Viadeo makes your job opportunity visible to active job seekers on the platform, to ensure that your recruitment process is successful. The social network service also enables you to manage the applications while minimizing recruitment costs.

8

Got A Question? Yahoo Answers!

Yahoo Answers is an ideal tool for any business that is looking to share expertise and knowledgeable insights with its target audience. Yahoo Answers lets you find questions pertinent to your niche and area of expertise, to which you can offer comprehensive answers. As a business, leveraging Yahoo Answers not only builds trust with your audience but can also help to drive traffic to your site and effectively to your business. In return, you will set yourself (and your brand) as the go-to person for solutions in your niche.

Setting Up Yahoo Answers For Business

To get started on Yahoo Answers, you need to register for an account. This will require you to sign up for a Yahoo email. Be sure to complete your profile page with the relevant information about you and your business. Remember that you are on the platform to offer your expertise and to build trust with your audience.

In addition to highlighting information about yourself, other users will also use your profile page to view your level of activity on the platform as well as the points you have earned for answering questions. Your profile also shows the questions you have asked, those you have answered and those that you found interesting.

Yahoo Answers allows you to include a link to your site and other social networks in your profile. Although these are no follow links, users can still use them to find your business site and to interact with you on others social platforms including Facebook and Twitter. While Yahoo Answers can help drive traffic to your business website, it may not be effective as a link building strategy.

After registering for an account and creating your profile, you are ready to answer questions. Navigate to the homepage and then use the search box to find questions to answers. Questions are usually open to answers for four days. Use the Advanced search to find niche specific questions by typing in relevant keywords.

Under the option 'Search for Keywords Match In', select 'Questions.' Then choose 'All' under the 'Category' option. Under the 'Question Status' option select 'Open Question,

Best Answer Has Not Been Chosen.' Select 'Any Time 'under the option 'Date Submitted', finally, select '% Thumbs Up Rating', and choose 'All Evaluations.'

Choose about 5 to 10 questions that you feel capable of answering. This will earn you 5 to 10 profile points and even though this might not have a direct impact on your brand visibility, it contributes to building your user status on the platform. Do not place links to your website or social profile in all the answers you give. This will keep Yahoo and other users from viewing your answers as spam. It is advisable that you include a link in the answer that is most comprehensive and best answered. Ideally create a landing page on your site providing a more detailed answer to their question and then send them there. It is also a good idea to answers questions in more than one related categories to interact with a greater audience.

Make use of the RSS feed to simplify your search. The feed feature allows you to easily filter through the categories on Yahoo Answers, by subscribing to specific categories and then receiving pertinent questions through the feed. For example, if you are an expert in marketing, you would select the 'Marketing' category and then subscribe to the RSS feed that will notify you about questions that need answers in this category.

Tip: Distinguish yourself from spammers by signing your name in your answers in addition to leaving your links.

People tend to read the answers at the top of the page. The best answers will drive greater traffic to your site as these answers are displayed at the top of the Answers page.

Building Your Community

Yahoo Answers allows you to expand your network by adding friends and inviting them to join the platform. You can send questions to people in your network and you can offer feedback to question answered by other users. When people in your network ask you questions, your answers will be displayed in your Yahoo Answers profile. As you build your network, invite people who are likely to ask high quality and pertinent questions especially those related to your niche. If you already have Twitter or Facebook connections with customers, be sure to invite them to interact with you on Yahoo Answers.

Yahoo Answers lets you answer questions that target location specific audiences. Use the Yahoo Answers

International option to answer questions origination from a specific location. This is especially important for businesses that are looking to attract localized traffic to their ad campaigns, as well as to their business websites. Addressing answers asked by people in your location offers you a competitive advantage over similar businesses in your area. Addressing people's concerns not only places you as a trustworthy expert and source of information, but also brings your brand along.

Yahoo Answers uses a points and levels system to encourage users to participate on the platform and to make use of the best practices. The actions you take will have an impact on your points and level. Points show other users your level of activity and the value of your answers. Some activities that will earn you points are signing up and participating, answering a question, having your answer chosen as the best or voting for an answer. While these points are not redeemable for a prize, they go a long way in demonstrating your expertise, attracting more people to your network and eventually boosting traffic to your site.

Building Your Website

In addition to driving traffic, leveraging Yahoo answers enables you to build your website as well. As you continue to engage in the platform, you will see that people are asking the same questions frequently. Use this pattern to find out more about interesting and popularly asked subjects in your niche or related niches. Use these questions or topics to create great blog posts that will not only offer relevant answers but will also interest your readers. Use the save option to keep track of any questions you want to explore further. You may also save these questions in your private list or RSS feed.

Additionally you can use the questions you have answered to create comprehensive articles, for submission to article directories and listings or even create videos that you can post on YouTube. As you may already know, both methods are valuable in creating authoritative backlinks to your website or blog.

9

Get Rated On Yelp!

Today Yelp is more of a necessity than it is an option for local small businesses. People in cities use Yelp to determine where to eat, where to hang out with friends and family and where to shop. As a local business owner, Yelp is an invaluable tool for creating local exposure for your business, tracking what people are saying about your brand and determining the needs of your local customers. This social tool allows businesses to integrate the power of social marketing and geo-location services. Here is how to get started:

Setting Up Yelp For Business

Setting up a business page on Yelp is free. First, find your business at the Yelp search box on the Business Page. Enter your business name, your location and then 'Search.' Yelp will look for related local business establishments and display a list of these businesses. When you find your business, click 'Unlock' to unlock your enterprise.

Next, create your account by filling requisite information such as your name, email address and password. This will be your login. Click 'Continue' to proceed with the application. Yelp requires you to answer a short automated call to verify your information. After the quick verification, you will have access to the Business Owners page and dashboard to edit you business profile. Keep your Yelp profile consistent with your business profile in other social networks.

Complete you profile by providing adequate details about your business. Remember that customers will come to your business pages to see what you are about and what you offer. Update your profile often.

Building A Yelp Community

Building a strong and loyal following community is integral to your success on Yelp. Your Yelp community will help you market your business by reviewing it and recommending it to their friends.

First, link your Yelp profile to your blog, business website and social networks. This will help you build a relationship with other Yelp users with the same interests as you. This approach will also link you with friends who are already on Yelp.

Next, find businesses that interest you and start to review them. Ensure that your reviews are genuine and valuable to other users. Particularly useful is to review new businesses you discover and send these businesses a message when you review them and you do not see a response. Reviewing other businesses will go a long way in establishing formidable business partnerships.

Also, look around to see consumers that are reviewing local businesses in your location and request them to become your 'friends' on Yelp. Use the talk section on Yelp to see local active users to engage. Consider that Yelpers are tech savvy, eager to spread news about their favorite business and are typically, social media influencers. Use the compliment link beneath each written review to complement the reviewer; this will make you more visible to active Yelpers and reviewers.

Then, embed the Yelp button on your blog and website. This will tell your site visitors that you are on Yelp and that they can connect with you there. The buttons can direct site visitors to your Yelp pages for them to see the reviews your business has received. If your site visitors are already on Yelp, then they can add you as their 'friend.'

Grow your community by integrating your Yelp business pages with Facebook and Twitter. Integration allows you to share reviews, announcement, promotions and events with your connections on other social networks. Integrating your Yelp profile with Twitter and Facebook also informs your followers and fans about your presence on Yelp and encourages them to become your 'friends' on the Yelp platform.

Yelp Community Management

As you build your community on Yelp, constructively engage with this community. An important aspect of community engagement is the management of customer reviews. Whether you receive positive or negative reviews, you need to insightfully respond to them.

You can respond to reviews privately or publicly. For positive reviews, simply say 'thank you', but do not offer to give them perks for positively reviewing your business. Respond to negative reviews by acknowledging the reviewers circumstances and if possible offer to address the matter. The public feedback tool is most effective for publishing information that concerns a majority of your followers, such as how you have addressed a specific issue. It is also helpful in clarifying any negative comment or false reviews.

Place a sign at your business premise to encourage visitors to offer Yelp reviews. If you offer online service, ask your clients and contacts to leave a review too. If some of your customers are not Yelpers yet, encourage them to join and engage in the network. Reviews will help to boost your Yelp page rankings at the local search engines.

Yelp Advertising

The monthly cost for small business advertising on Yelp ranges between $300 and $1,000. Businesses featured on the advertising program have more exposure at the site search engines; this allows users to find you easily for related searches.

The Yelp advertisement program also allows you to feature a review of your choice at the top of your business page. Users looking for related business will see this review first.

Yelp Events And Announcements

Yelp makes it possible for local businesses to announce promotions, offers and events and to reach a wide audience at a minimal cost. Whether you have opened a new shop, offering a seasonal discount or hosting a local event, Yelp lets you create a deal or event and to publish it on your business page. Using the announcement tool will also make you more visible in related Yelp search results.

Yelp sends a weekly newsletter highlighting events, promotions and announcements to users. Additionally, users around your location may be notified of any promotions or events your business is offering or hosting, prompting the potential customer to check in to your business. Make your announcements and offers unique and helpful to Yelpers.

To determine if your city is eligible for a Yelp event visit http://yelp.com/events and then click on the 'Other Cities' button to look for your city.

Yelp will then direct you to a page that will enable you to create an event. Enter the location of your business, website, event details and photos. Leverage the 'What and Why' box to market and promote your event. Use relevant keywords (related to your business and the event) in the description box to optimize your event for related searches at the site search box.

Engage Yelpers with the event by inviting them to 'Discuss this event.' Use the 'Send to Friend' tab to invite Yelpers and connections in other social networks to the Event. Continue to update those whom you have invited and have responded saying 'I'm In'.

Build a relationship with those who attended by interacting with them after the event - they might become loyal, buying customers.

An example of local business using Yelp to drive traffic and sales is a small restaurant in Waltham, Massachusetts, *In a Pickle*. The business has more than 222 reviews and an impressive 4 star rating. According to the business owner, 40% of its new customers are Yelpers.

10

Ning: Your Very Own Social Networking Site Today

Ning is a social networking platform with more than 40 million users and over 2 million networks. This web-based service allows you to create your brand social network and to actively engage with the people in your network. The members in each network create their own profiles, connect with friends, share content and engage in community discussions. Why would a business want to create a social network when there are so many other social communities like Facebook, Twitter, Pinterest and Google+? Because, when you are in charge of your community, your brand becomes an integral part of this your network. You are in charge of the content, you can easily interact with new customers, and you can use a single platform to host a real and dynamic community.

Setting Up Ning For Business

To get started on Ning, create an account by visiting the site's homepage. You have 30 days to try it out for free and then you need to choose between one of three service levels they offer.

Ning requires you to enter basic information including your name, email address and password. You will also be requested to create a Ning URL i.e. thenameofyourgroup.ning.com.

After the registration process click on the 'Create Your Own Social Network' tab to start your community. Offer a detailed description of your group to tell other users what your social network will be about. Of course, you are looking to create a social community based on your brand and niche industry. Include a compelling tagline in your group description and then select the relevant keywords that will identify your social network. Use terms that others who want to join the network are likely to use when looking for your network.

Next, customize your group profile. Choose features for your community including a blog, forum, themed groups, videos, music, chat features, reminders, applications and RSS feeds. The features you select to place in your network largely depend on the level of interaction you are looking to obtain in the network. Some features may be relevant for one social network and not so for another.

Design your profile. You have control over where features will appear on the social network interface. Select a theme for your network site and then customize it to reflect your business and personal branding, for example by using colors that reflect your brand. Remember to add a link to your site and other social networks.

Click on 'Launch' to activate your Ning social network. You will receive an email showing you how to start building your community. Ning will crawl your email contacts to find anyone who is already on Ning to enable you to include them in your network.

Integrating With Other Social Networks

Ning allows you to connect your social network to other social communities including Facebook and Twitter. Integration is one of the best ways to build your community on Ning and allowing users (and yourself) to share content across the Web.

Facebook: When you integrate your social network on Ning with Facebook, your network members can easily share content with their fans and friends on Facebook. Users can share status updates, discussions, events, videos and blogs as well as photo. This cross sharing with other networks serves to boost your brand visibility not just among Ning users but also with other social communities on Facebook.

Twitter: Integrating your Ning with Twitter allows you and your network users to publish on Twitter, the updates and content you post on the Ning network.

Ning Apps: These are third-party services, which enable you to interact better with your network members. The applications give access to features such as YouTube for Video, chats, platforms for hosting events and selling tickets and an advertisement space for members in your network for example for business members.

Ning Analytics

Ning allows you to measure the effectiveness of your social engagement and strategy on the platform. Ning lets you integrate your social network with Google Analytics to gain insights into traffic sources and the effectiveness of your content.

Using Ning For Branding

One of the most attractive features about Ning is that it allows you to create a community around anything. This gives you the freedom to target your customers and to bring them to one network where you can have better engagement with them and they too can identify with your brand. Here are a few ways you can use Ning to make your brand more visible to your target audience:

Use It To Engage With Your Community: Ning enables you to create a community in which people talk about niche specific issues that interest them. It is important that you make use of this 'chat and discussion' aspect of Ning to see what people are saying about your brand. However, you too should engage in the conversation - contribute to forum discussions and answer pertinent questions and issues. Keep the conversation going by regularly posting relevant and interesting content and encourage others to do the same.

Use Ning To Build A Greater Audience: Ning members can belong to more than one network. Ning also has a

News Feed similar to Facebook that allows you to see the interaction of other users with your brand. Thus, in addition to that one user interacting with your account, their friends too can join and engage with your network. It is also likely that the people who have an interest in your niche and live live in your community, might be checking in to your physical business soon.

Use It To Host Meet-ups And Events: Ning is a valuable platform for gathering people with similar interests and bringing them together. After an offline event, you can continue the discussion online. Ning enables you to integrate your offline activities with your online presence. Go ahead and host industry specific events in your neighborhood or in your business premise to grow your brand visibility and to engage with your audience.

Customer Service: As all businesses know, customer service is integral to business success. Ning offers a great environment for customers to provide you feedback about your brand and product/service offering. In this way, you can immediately address their concerns, see what they are proposing and take steps to making the required changes.

11

Play The Klout Game And Become An Influencer

Klout is one of the most popular tools that businesses and marketers use to measure the effectiveness of their social media campaign. As a business leveraging different social networks, Klout measures your influence on these networks. Klout has more than 100 million users and can be a valuable tool for measuring and improving your online visibility. In addition to helping you boost your online visibility, this tool is valuable in finding influential people in your field and rewarding customers who boost your brand.

Klout determines users' score based on three primary metrics, which include:

True Reach: This is a measurement of the number of people you influence as well as the number of people the people you influence are linked to. True Reach tells you a lot about the nature of your network, how expansive or limited it is, and how you are connected to your audience. How is 'True Reach' relevant to your business? This metric tells you if you are reaching your target audience and if the connection you have with them is effective or needs improvement. It also tells you whether you need to work on expanding your network.

Amplification: This measurement offers you insight about the effectiveness of your content or message. Is your message driving action, getting people to talk about your brand or product? Amplification is an important metric as it offers you information about the type of content or topic that makes you more influential and that excites your audience. A high amplification metric show you that your message is having the desired impact, while a low one indicates the need to tailor your message to fit your audience's needs.

Facebook: likes, shares and comments

Twitter: retweets and mentions

Google+: +1s, reshares and comments

Foursquare: to-dos and tips

Network Impact: This metric tells you about the influence of those in your network. The more influential your network, the more of an asset it is for your brand marketing. By having more influencers in your network, you can leverage their influence to make your brand more visible online, to prospects and key contacts in your industry.

Setting Up Klout For Business

If you are a Twitter or Facebook user, Klout automatically creates an account for you based on the public information in your Twitter/Facebook profile. Some essential features on Klout are useful as you leverage this tool for your brand:

The Dashboard: This page shows the different social networks that are integrated to your Klout account including Twitter, Facebook, LinkedIn, and Google+, among others (see screenshots below for a complete list). On this dashboard you can also find your score fluctuations.

Coming Soon!

We're actively working with many other networks to be able to gauge your influence everywhere on the web. Stay tuned!

Klout Score: This is one of the most important aspects of your interaction with Klout. The Klout Score is an indication of your influence across the social networks that you participate in. At the score area, you will also see a summary of the people who influence you and the areas or topics in which you have the greatest influence. This is especially helpful as it allows you to identify and engage with key contacts in your field. Also, knowing the area which you have the greatest influence enables you to determine the content and message that your audience is receiving well. All the screenshots are taken from Mashable's dashboard. They have a Klout score of 66.

Mashable

The largest independent website dedicated to news & resources for the connected generation. Tweets from @mashable staff. Send questions/comments to @mashablehq.

Influences 843K others

tweet · see more...

Influential about 20 topics

- +K Technology
- +K Social Media
- +K Media

tweet · see all...

Score Analysis: The score analysis shows you an info-graph about your Klout score. It displays the trends of your score over a given period as well as the activities that have an impact on your Klout score. The score analysis also shows your history based on the primary metrics that include true reach, amplification and network impact.

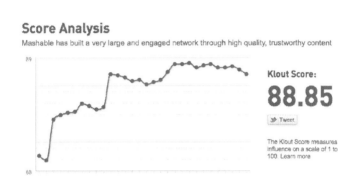

Topics: This feature shows the area you are most influential in. Klout automatically aggregates topics related to the content and messages you have been sending across the social networks. If some of the topics where you feel you are most influential are not generated, you can add the topics using the +K feature. Understanding your area of influence provides you insight on the effectiveness of your content and techniques to better engage your target audience.

Mashable is influential about 20 topics

Technology
Give +K
Recent +K
STRONG
Get more +K Tweet • share

Social Media
Give +K
Recent +K
STRONG
Get more +K Tweet • share

Media
Give +K
Recent +K
STRONG
Get more +K Tweet • share

Blogging
Give +K
Recent +K

Klout Style: This feature offers you a description of your social media engagements. The tool uses a 4 by 4 matrix to gauge your social interactions against that of the people who influence you. This feature assigns you a style such a 'Networker' if you are actively engaged in meeting the right people and offering your audience relevant content. Mashable is a 'Celebrity', which means that they are very influential in the social media world. Other styles are: 'Curator', 'Broadcaster', 'Taste Maker', 'Celebrity', etc. To get the full description of each style I recommend downloading the presentation from http://slideshare.net/amover/klout-styles.

Mashable is a Celebrity

You can't get any more influential than this. People hang on your every word, and share your content like no other. You're probably famous in real life and your fans simply can't get enough.

Influencers: This tool further shows you the details of the people you influence and those who influence you. You also receive insights on your connections with them through other social network. This is helpful as it allows you to engage closely with your audience as well as your key influencers. Key influencers can be businesses in your niche, key contacts such as journalists and bloggers or customers who have a great ability to influence others into action. Other details include the influencers' Klout score and the activities that influence their followers.

Perks: Businesses offer perks to their most influential customers. By offering perks, you are not only rewarding your influential customers, but you are also leveraging their ability to influence, to market and promote your brand and product offering. Look at perks as special offers that you give to users who know people, are actively engaged in social networking and love your brand/product.

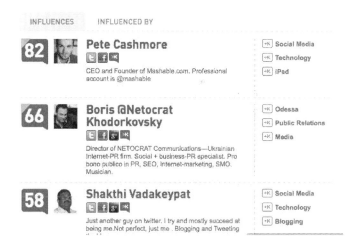

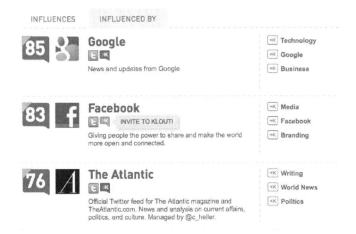

Klout Brand Pages

Klout brand pages enable businesses to leverage Klout not as individuals but as brands. As a result, brands, like individuals, can have a Klout Score based on their influence in their specific niches. Brand pages also make it possible for businesses to actively and closely interact with influential businesses in their topical industry.

Additionally, Klout brand pages allow you to **display your content streams** to be viewed by other users. This serves to place your own brand in front of an audience that is important to your business. Integration to other popular social networks allows you to communicate directly with influential people in your network. One of the most valuable features of Klout brand pages is that **it shows your top 10 influencers** and **the perks you could get for being an influencer of their brand**. These people are influential and dedicated to your business. By knowing who they are and how to engage with them, you have the opportunity to capitalize on their influence to make your brand more visible. See below an example of a Klout Brand Page from Trident.

Top Trident Content

Using The +K Feature

The +K is similar to the +1 on Google+ or 'Like' on Facebook. This feature enables you to vote for the content posted or activity carried out by the influencers you are connected to. By giving a +K you are telling that person that you find their content interesting. See below the many rewards Mashable received from sharing useful and relevant content. Note that every day there are about 50,000 +Ks exchanged between Klout users.

Mashable earned 38 achievements!

The +K is a great way to acknowledge the influential people in your network, to provide them with feedback and to make yourself more visible to them. Keep in mind that one of the reasons a business uses Klout is to meet influential people who can assist in improving their online brand visibility.

Each day, when you log into your Klout account, you receive 10 +K. To offer a +K to the people who influence you simply click on their topics page and then select the option 'Give +K' next to the topic that has influenced you.

You can use the +K feature to create your own topic or offer others a topic but this will take up 5 of your +Ks at once. You too can improve the number of +Ks that you receive from other members, by creating relevant and interesting content for your audience. This will help to boost your influence and eventually your score.

Benefits Of Leveraging Klout For Business

a) Personal Branding: Your interactions on these social networks will determine your influence and effectively, your brand's online visibility.

b) Social Media Measurement: In addition to determining your own social media influence, Klout enables you to measure your client's influence and level of social engagement. Why should a business determine their clients' level of influence in social networks? Influential customers are integral to your business as a marketing and promotional channel. Influential clients are certainly great at networking, are always abreast with trends and know how to spread the word about a product they like.

c) Integration With Others Social Networks: Klout makes it easy to track the effectiveness of your social campaign in the various networks that you are. This integration lets you see how you are interacting with each social platform and how you can improve these interactions. That said you should only link your Klout account to networks in which you are active. An inactive social network account will reflect negatively on your Klout Score. While Klout can help you measure your influence in most social networks, it works best with Twitter. Klout will tell you if you need to cut back on posting links and engage more with your audience or if you need to expand your network and social activities.

d) Rewarding Influencers: After identifying influencers through their Klout scores, you want to engage with them and keep them close. Klout allows you to create and offer perks to these influencers. Clients like to be recognized and awarded for patronizing their favorite brands. Placing your products in the hands of few influencers can help to significantly improve your brand awareness.

Perks on Klout fall under different categories allowing you to create and offer rewards depending on your niche. Some popular categories include retail, experiences, food beverages, technology, sports and entertainment. In addition to rewarding influencers, Perks offer a valuable platform for launching products, product sampling, as well as product development and experimenting.

Some example of businesses that using the Perks feature on Klout to identify and reward their influencers include:

Chilis: Chilis offers gift cards to encourage their top influencers to purchase light menu choices and to try the 2 for $20 steak dinner.

PopChips: Encourages its influential clients to sample its different flavors. They send (via mail) 6 different flavors to their top influencers.

These and other businesses offer perks to their select influencers with the anticipation that the influencers will tell other people about the brand and product offering. Influencers are not obliged to talk about a brand that offers them perks, but they will certainly be inclined to talk about you if they like your product.

So How Do You Find Influencers?

The Klout interface features various topics including marketing, money, entertainment and religion. Click on any topic to see more information about that topic and the people associated with that topic. To find relevant influencers, select topics related to your niche and begin to interact with them from the social platform that both of you are connected to.

As You Leverage Klout For Your Business, What Exactly Should You Be Measuring?

The simple approach is to pay attention to the topics that you are most influential in or those that are related to your business. If you are in marketing, you want to measure your influence on marketing topics and those topics related to the marketing niche. One of the best things about Klout is that you can easily post your content and then find your influential topics through the dashboard without the need to use special features like hashtags. You will know that your social media strategy is effective when your Klout Score and Influence grow.

Check Klout's blog at http://corp.klout.com/blog/ for great tips on how to enhance your experience not only on their own platform but also on other social media sites. See below two screenshots from their blog.

When You Receive +K, How Do You Respond?

"I always respond and thank the person. If I know them well, I will do a public tweet and frequently return the favor with a +K. If I don't know them well or have never engaged with them, I may send them a thank you via a DM."

Alan K'necht
Partner - Analytics & Social Marketing at Digital Always Media Inc.
@aknecht

"Klout +K's are a great way to learn about people and show your appreciation for their influence. When I receive a +K from someone, I send out a 'Thank You' tweet. I then go to the person's Klout page and look to see what topics they have listed so I can give them a +K back in a topic that best describes them."

Lori Kober
Social Butterfly/Social Media Curator
@Lori_SF

"95% of the time, I will respond with +K for them. If we have some type of relationship, I will select a topic that I would consider them to have some expertise in. If I am not familiar with them, I will likely pick the most rated topic for them as it give me an opportunity to keep a closer eye on the content they socialize on."

Jonathan Long
Social Media Manager at Seagate
@Weezul

"I usually thank them and reciprocate. However, when I tweet it out I change the message from the standard to something more personal."

Andy Gonzalez
Director of Community Management at Speak Social
@AndyViral

KLOUT

What Social Network Do You Use the Most?

"At this point in time, **Facebook is the Social Media hub.** Most social media networks out there [Instagram, Foursquare, Pinterest, etc.] can cross post to Facebook directly from their mobile apps. The posting on Facebook may entice one's followers to join the new network."

Benedict Corpuz
Flying Geek/Social Media Addict
@SuperBen

"Since signing up for Instagram in November 2010, the way I look at the world around me has changed. Instagram is a digital canvas for every beautiful moment of my life and the platform that allows me to share those moments with the world."

Ross Sheingold
Brand Channel Manager, Social Media Strategist
@RossSheingold

"I've used Twitter more than any other social network. **It gives me the ability to access information and communicate with multiple communities that I'm involved with.** This ensures that Twitter gets more of my attention than any other platform."

Tim Welsh
Digital Brand Management Specialist
@TWel5

"While most students spend their "free time" on Facebook, I put my free time to use by networking on Twitter [I've been offered internships based soley on my Twitter presence!]. **I've been able to prove my worth as a writer, a community manager, and professional 140 characters at a time.**"

Adam Britten
Master of Digital Marketing Student
@AdamBritten

"**My most used network is Twitter since I am able to quickly engage and interact with individuals on any given topic.** Sharing information, photos, videos and web links is trackable and easily spread to a wide community using key hashtags."

12
Guide To Social Link Building

Social link building is an integral component of your online visibility and social marketing strategy. Inbound links from authoritative and pertinent sites indicate that your own website has quality content for your audience. Creating links makes you visible to key contacts in your niche, builds trust between you and your customers/audience and boosts your personal brand as an expert in your field. Here is how you can optimize your online visibility through social link building:

Creating Social Profiles

Social media sites are valuable platforms for link building at a low cost. Although the value of social links is still contentious among SEO and social media professionals, you can find effective ways to leverage the power of these networks.

There are different types of social media sites and I only listed below the ones I use on a daily basis:

Social Networking Sites: Facebook, Twitter, Google+, Linkedin, Xing, Ecademy, CafeMom

Curation Sites: Pinterest, Storify, Paper.li, Scoop.it

Social Bookmarking/Tagging: StumbleUpon, Del.icio.us, Digg, Reddit

Social Publishing Sites: Squidoo, Hubpages, Ning

Video Sharing Sites: Youtube, Vimeo, Viddler

Photo Sharing Sites: Flickr, Instagram, PhotoBucket

Blogs: WordPress, Blogger

Microblogs: Twitter, Tumblr, Posterious

Documents Sharing: Scribd, SlideShare

Personal Broadcasting: LiveStream, UStream, Blog Talk Radio

Reviews: Yelp, Epinions, Amazon, eBay, TripAdvisor, Lonely Planet Forums, Angie's List

Social Q&As: Linkedin Answers, Quora, Yahoo! Answers, Answers.com, Sprouter,

Social Events: Linkedin Events, EventBrite

Location Based Networks: Google+ Local, Gowalla, Foursquare, Facebook Places

Group Buying: Groupon, Living Social, Crowdsavings

Create a profile on all the main social networks, personalize your URL with your business name (socialnetwork.com/yourbusinessname) and then link them to your tweetdeck.com, hootsuite.com, sproutsocial.com or seesmic.com accounts. These sites will allow you to schedule and post on multiple social platforms from a single dashboard. It is also recommended that you ping the URL of a web page each time you posted new content for a faster indexing by the search engines. To do this you can use pingler.com.

Facebook: Facebook offers a wide and active audience that provides a great opportunity for linking. Link building on Facebook entails interacting with the people who are already in your network, either for reciprocal or one-way links to your site. You will be surprised at how willing your connections on Facebook are to link to your site when you simply ask them to.

Consider establishing a Fan Page for your business and then ask your friends to join the page. Post promotions, special offers and coupons, or articles related to your business or niche. This way, people will link to your site as they share this information with their connections on Facebook.

Twitter: Twitter is also a valuable tool that allows you to connect and engage with other users. Even though the level of connection on Twitter is sometimes fleeting, you can follow and engage key contacts in your niche and from this relationship, they can mention you and link to your website.

Twitter allows you to embed your website URL in your posts and updates. This way, those who follow you can go directly to your website, learn about your business and link back to your website if it offers high quality and relevant content.

LinkedIn: unlike Facebook and Twitter, you can greatly grow your connections on LinkedIn. You can send InMail to the people you are connected to. A paid LinkedIn account also lets you send InMail to people who are not directly connected with. InMail is a great way to reach people because it has a high opening rate. The 'InMail' simply introduces people to your business and if they like what they see, they might link back to you.

Pinterest: the 'Popular' section on Pinterest will show you the most popular images; these are typically original and compelling. When you post unique pictures on your board, other users are more likely to repin, like and comment on them. Coupons and QR codes are valuable tools to use in attracting an audience and get repinned. This engagement goes a long way in making your brand more popular on the social site. Users can also comment on content pinned by other users as well share this content across the site and on other social networking platforms.

If you are interested in digging deeper into the Pinterest topic, you may want to purchase The Ultimate Guide To Marketing Your Business With Pinterest. This book is the only definitive guide you'll ever need to discover Pinterest, the web's latest social networking phenomenon that has the potential to be a better marketing tool than Facebook and Twitter.

The Ultimate Guide To Marketing Your Business With...

A Practical Toolkit To Unlock The Web's Latest Social Networking Phenomenon

GABRIELA TAYLOR

YouTube: like other social networking sites, YouTube has an active community in which people interact, share ideas, leave comments, ask questions and share content. By commenting on other people's videos, they get to know that you exist. This is also a great opportunity to showcase your expertise and to attract people to what you have to offer. Look around for groups in your niche or those that your local customers and prospects are likely to be in. Join and interact with people in these groups and soon you will have the opportunity to introduce them to your business. Always direct viewers to your site after they watch the video. Embedding a link to your site is just the beginning of the conversion process, from viewer to potential lead. In addition, you may create an independent landing page within your site for users who visit your website from YouTube. You may use this landing page to showcase product/service offering or to capture visitors' information for list building.

Google+: leverage the effectiveness of the + 1 option. You can place this sharing button in your website, in ads and in your content too. Whenever a user +1s the content you distribute to them, they create an endorsement for your brand. The content is also shareable with others in the user's Circle. Placing the +1 button in your content will go a long way in allowing your audience to engage with your brand.

Host a hangout for your customers and those in your Circles. Leverage the power of Hangouts to have question and answer sessions with your local community and customers. You will be surprised by how much your customers appreciate getting their questions answered especially before making a purchasing decision.

Use Ripple to see how users interact with the content that you post. Ripples not only allow you to connect with Google+ influencers, but also to see how your content is shared on the platform. Visit the Ripples page to see the most influential followers for each of the posts that you send out. Influencers in your Google+ network are essential as they can help you spread the word not just about your posts but also about your brand and product offering.

If you are interested in digging deeper into topics such as YouTube or Google+, you may want to purchase The Ultimate Guide To Building And Marketing Your Business With Google. Learn more about the full suite of Google tools, how you can use them to launch and grow your business and have a successful online strategy by understanding exactly what you can get from Google.

The Ultimate Guide To Building And Marketing Your Business With ...

Google

A Step By Step Guide To Unlocking The Power Of Google Tools And Maximizing Your Online Potential

GABRIELA TAYLOR

Tumblr: Blogs on other platforms such as WordPress, Blogger or within your website, tend to be longer. Tumblr audiences are less inclined to these types of traditional blogs, instead preferring to read, follow, like and reblog shorter, snappier posts. Nevertheless, this does not mean that you cannot leverage the Tumblr audience back to your post and allow them to see the type of content that you offer on your comprehensive blog. A good approach to take is to post shorter versions of your blog posts onto Tumblr and then insert a link or two that will direct users back to your comprehensive post/site. This way, readers who find your post interesting might be able to link back their own Tumblr or fuller blogs to your post.

If you are interested in digging deeper into the Tumblr topic, you may want to purchase The Ultimate Guide To Marketing Your Business With Tumblr. Throughout this book, I will show you how Tumblr can be utilized as a fantastic tool to showcase your brand to a worldwide audience.

The Ultimate Guide To Marketing Your Business With...

Using Tumblr To Leverage Social Buzz And Develop A Brand Awareness Strategy For Your Business

GABRIELA TAYLOR

Increase the number of people who read, follow and link to your blog by integrating your blog to your Facebook, Twitter, LinkedIn or other social networks where you have a profile. Twitterfeed.com is a tool that could help you achieve this. Your blog posts will be published automatically on your chosen social networks and your readers would be able to link back to your site or blog. Also do not forget adding social buttons to each page on your site to increase the number of Likes, Shares, Pins, +1s or +Ks.

Social Meet-ups: Do not let your social link building start and end online. Attend meet ups and conferences to meet key people in your field. Remember that networking and getting the right connections is at the heart of link building. At these local conferences, you will gain insight about other people's businesses and thus the opportunities available for you. Meeting and interacting face to face with your potential partners is much more valuable than sending them an email or phoning them to inquire about a link building opportunity.

Submitting And Publishing Guest Posts

Guest blogging has the capacity to furnish you with high quality links, if you take the time to select your guest blogging partners. In fact compared to social networks, guest blogging may offer higher quality links. Here are some best practices for guest blog posting:

Build your portfolio: When you contact a blog owner or a guest blogging platform for the opportunity to post, they will want to see your content. If you are just getting started, use your blog as your portfolio. The type of content to submit is different for each guest blog platform. Pay attention to the requirements to improve the chances of your content being accepted. Overall, all authoritative guest blogs require high quality and relevant content.

Find the best guest blogging opportunities:

MyBlogGuest.com: it's a great site that links content creators to blog owners and journalists. It has about 28,000 users from around the world (see screenshot below) and places daily around 200 articles.

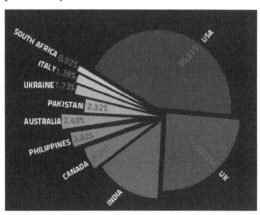

It also gives you the opportunity to personalize your profile by linking it to your other social media sites.

MyBlogGuest.com offers three levels of service to choose from:

Features	Free	Basic Premium	Advanced
		$30 per month	$70 per month
		Subscribe	Subscribe
Access to all available guest blogging opportunities (through the forum)	✓	✓	✓
Social media (and other) help from board administrators and moderators	✓	✓	✓
The ability to offer your blogs to host available articles in the Article Gallery	✓	✓	✓
The ability to upload new articles to Articles Gallery for hundreds of bloggers to offer their sites to publish your content	-	4 Articles Live in the Gallery	16 Articles Live in the Gallery
The ability to upload new infographics to Infographic Gallery to earn easy buzz around your infographics	-	✓	✓
The ability to track all your published articles status (we monitor all your published article and notify you if it was deleted, links removed or nofollowed)	-	✓	✓
The ability to manage and track your contacts and tasks via the "Watch list"	-	✓	✓
The ability to send guest posts directly to blogger's wp-admin (save time! no emailing back and forth!)	-	3 a day	3 a day
The ability to receive guest posts directly to your wp-admin as drafts from approved members (save time! no emailing back and forth!)	✓	✓	✓
Access to private forums for advanced / secret guest blogging and link building tips	-	✓	✓
The ability to receive email digest of new threads, blogs and articles within any category	-	✓	✓
The option to subscribe to weekly email digest within any category or categories (to get alerted of new offers, blogs and articles)	-	✓	✓
Daily PM + Forum email limit	20	40	60
		Subscribe	Subscribe

Guestblogit.com: it's a guest blog market place where you can submit monthly one article for free. Then publishers will pick it up and publish it on their sites. You can also subscribe to their paid version where you will be paying $20 per month for 5 articles submissions and many other extras that are listed in the screenshot below.

The Plan Features:	Free Member Free	* Pro Member $20
# Live Articles Allowed In Market	1	5
Be Rated	⚙	⚙
Be Reviewed	⚙	⚙
Rate Others	⚙	⚙
Send/Receive Direct Messages	⚙	⚙
Article Queue	⚙	⚙
Free Blog Engage Membership ($9.99 value)	⚙	⚙
Access To Promotion Svc	⚙	⚙
Custom Widgets/Badges	⚙	⚙
Become A Member Now!	REGISTER FREE!	SUBSCRIBE NOW!

Google: Use the Google search engine to find relevant guest posts in your niche. Simply search for various keywords (with quotes) such as 'write for us', 'guest post', 'guest blog', 'guest blog submission', 'guest post by', 'accepting guest posts' or 'guest post guidelines', preferably accompanied by a niche term.

Twitter: Use the Twitter search engine to find guest blogging opportunities posted on Twitter. Use a variation of the keywords used in your Google search.

Check websites in your niche: Use tools such as Open Site Explorer to look at the back links that the websites in your niche receive. This is will tell you about the guest blogging sites that the blog/website owners participate in.

Blogs: Look out for blogs that include the author bio and website URL at the beginning of the content. Blogs that will add the author bio and URL within the post as well as those providing a link to a website or social network profiles.

For more ideas on where to submit your content, I suggest checking two great Internet resources:

100 sites to submit guest posts

500 places to syndicate your content

What to look for in a site that accepts guest blogs:

Page Rank: Use tool such as SEOquake or SEO Site Tools to find out how the site ranks on Google search engines.

Domain Authority: Use a tool such as SEOmoz Toolbar for Chrome and Firefox to determine the site's domain authority.

Subscribers: These are site followers from Twitter, Facebook, Pinterest, Google+, YouTube and other social networking sites as well as those who have subscribed to the site RSS feed.

Traffic: Use Alexa Ranking to determine the amount of traffic the blog attracts. A lower number on Alexa indicates higher traffic. Google Ad Planner can also give you insights into the number of visitors to the site.

Running Promotional Contests

Hosting online competitions can help you attract links from various domains, key contacts (such as press publications) and authority sites.

Basic contests and promotions entail asking users to visit your website, to enter their details, answer a question and then finally determining the winner. The type of prize that you give away largely depends on you profit margins and bottom line.

By partnering with others in your industry to host the contest or promotion, you will not only gain publicity but also backlinks. In making their audience aware of the contest or promotion, your partners will mention you on their sites, thereby driving free traffic to your own site. You may also endorse other people's contests or promotions by offering additional prizes, in exchange for a link.

Make use of competition lists to list your contest/promotion. These sites will definitely link back to your site as they refer participants to your landing pages. Although your competition might take a few days before being listed, it is still worthwhile to leverage these sites. Good competition sites to look at are Loquax.co.uk, ThePrizeFinder.com and CompetitionWinner.com.au.

Send your competition to loyal Twitter followers, bloggers or any key contact you may know and who will not mind covering the contest or promotion. This will help you gain publicity, generate traffic and a few good links to your website.

Leverage the shareable nature of videos to make your contest/promotion more visible. Use platforms such as YouTube and Flickr to publish your videos and include a link to your website. Allow people to share the video across other social networking sites such as Facebook, Tumblr, and Pinterest and within YouTube too. The more people share and mention your promotional video, the more backlinks you are likely to generate.

Link up with local publications including newspapers and magazines with an online presence. These publications are usually willing to mention your contest or promotion in their website, thereby offering you an authoritative back link.

Submitting Articles To Article Directories

Article submission to authoritative directories and listings is an excellent technique to drive targeted and free traffic to your blog or website. Some of the most known article directories are: ehow.com, squidoo.com, hubpages.com, ezinearticles.com, examiner.com, technorati.com, gather.com and ideamarketers.com. Article directories have different requirements for the content they accept on their listing. High quality and well-written articles are generally accepted.

Pay attention to the keyword requirements. Avoid stuffing your article with keywords and instead strategically place them in the article title, meta description and article body. Use a tool such as Textalyzer to check your keyword density, which should be between two to five percent.

Here are some factors to consider when looking for suitable directories and listings for link building:

It is built for human use: The main aim of a directory should not be to solely optimize your rankings. Check to see if the site owner is especially active on blogs, forums and social communities. Such a site is most likely engineered for pure SEO purposes and not for human use. It is unlikely that this site will provide you a high quality link.

Selective: Sites that offer high quality links are typically hard to get in. Such directories have editors who review submitted articles before publishing them on the site. Examples of selective directories are Nature.com, Forbes Best of the Web and About.com.

High ranking: The sites that offer valuable links are those that rank well for the search terms that they target. A site that cannot rank well for its own title tags will not provide you the visibility that your articles deserve.

Associated with a trusted domain: Directories and listings that have their own domain may not always offer high quality links. However, those that are part of successful, well-known and trusted sites are more likely to provide you with high quality back links.

13

Top Social Networks For Entrepreneurs

In addition to putting your own efforts in building your business, there is a need to network with other entrepreneurs. Social networking platforms for entrepreneurs help you discover new opportunities and introduce you to novel ideas for addressing challenges in your niche. Here are some social networking tools to help you connect and engages with other entrepreneurs:

StartUp.com

StartUp is a social network that allows you to meet potential business partners with whom you can grow your business. It also offers a suitable environment for marketing your brand and making product sales, gaining useful insights into creating and delivering sales pitches, and establishing and growing an online business. The network provides a platform for members to interact with each other, exchange business opportunities and offer solutions to problems facing businesses, in the form of marketing and consultation services.

Ecademy.com

Ecademy is a membership-based network that attracts businesses and entrepreneurs who are looking for local and global connections. The network, which is primarily a resources that offers access to global networking events and techniques for leveraging social media, works on the philosophy of Know Me, Like Me, Follow Me. This philosophy is geared to help members maximize their bottom line, make the best use of social media and use online networking techniques to boost a brand. This is one of the oldest social networking platforms and offers a truly diverse resource base for small and medium enterprises.

MeetUp.com

MeetUp is a social networking tool that allows groups and individuals to integrate their offline experience with social media. This network enables you to create your own groups based on interests or industry affiliation and to invite like-minded people to exchange ideas offline and online. You can also join existing groups that appeal to your interest. The most attractive element of Meetup is that it is local as much as it is global. In this way, you can get together with local industry experts, businesses and prospects, hold offline events and continue the conversation online. Simply enter your city or zip code and MeetUp will show you various relevant meet-ups in your location.

MeetTheBooss.tv

MeetTheBoss is a free and resourceful platform that offers wide-ranging interviews with local and global business leaders. The interviews cover areas including businesses challenges and solutions to these challenges, strategies for business, and influential people in the world of business. The platform also offers a management-training program, and provides career and business advice to help you grow your business.

PROskore.com

PROskore is an online social network that measures your social influence and reputation. The score you receive helps you find new business opportunities among other network members. This network brands itself as the first social networking platform to measure professional influence as one interacts with social media. PROskore uses three metrics to determine ones influence. These include the social influence you have in other social networks, your level of activity based on the connections you make on PROskore, and your professional experience. There are over 200,000 members on the network who connect with each other on the basis on interest, industry affiliation as well as location.

Ryze.com

Ryze assists people to grow their businesses through expanding their social network. In addition to finding new opportunities and meeting new prospects, Ryze helps you meet up with past friends and contacts. The network offers its members a free profile/ homepage from where they can send messages to fellow members. As a member of Ryze, you can join Groups related to your niche as well as those based in your location. This network has a global membership of over 500,000 members from 200 countries and over 1000 organizations host networking Groups on this platform.

eConnect.Entrepreneur.com

Entrepreneur Connect is part of Entrepreneur Magazine, a subsidiary of Entrepreneur Media. This network was specifically created for small businesses and entrepreneurs. Entrepreneur Connect allows you to develop your profile, interact with other community members, and exchange ideas. This network is however not too keen on self-promotion and instead looks to encourage entrepreneurs to share ideas that will assist fellow members. This is an ideal network if you are looking to link up with suppliers, service providers for your business, niche experts and past contacts. In addition to creating new groups or joining existing ones, you can create your own blog, which may appear on the network's homepage.

PerfectBusiness.com

If you are looking to engage with a large group of focused experts, entrepreneurs and investors from a wide range of industries, the Perfect Business could be the ideal networking environment. The Perfect Business attracts potentially big clients, investors, (if you are looking to expand your business) as well as business partners who can help you take your business to the next level of growth. The network features a video center, which gives you access to a wide resource base of entrepreneurial insight. Other benefits include investor center and business plan software to help you build a successful business. The network has both free and paid membership, which costs $29.99 monthly.

Biznik.com

While many people compare Biznik to LinkedIn, Biznik says that it is a social networking platform that 'does not suck.' This social network attracts self-employed people, CEOs and freelancers. The platform allows you to exchange ideas, provide and receive advice and expand your business opportunities. All members are required to use their real name and data. The editors at Biznik look through all the profiles to ensure that names and data are real. The network offers free membership, an active membership that costs $10 for an advanced profile and a supporting membership that costs $24 for improved profile visibility.

UpSpring.com

Upspring was created with the aim of helping small businesses and brands meet their marketing objectives through social networking. The platform enables entrepreneurs to leverage the power of networks such as Google+, Facebook and Twitter to grow their prospect and customers bases.

PartnerUp.com

Partner Up is a free networking platform that attracts businesses, co-founders, executives, partners and board members. This network offers an environment, which allows you to ask questions, offer advice, locate professional service providers such as accountants for your business and suitable real estate property. The network also allows businesses to advertise their product/service offering.

Efactor.com

Efactor brands itself as the largest network of entrepreneurs that helps small businesses find funding to grow their enterprises, gain knowledge, minimize business costs and expand their revenue bases. The network offers its members access to discounted business tools, offline and online business events and an environment for exchanging ideas and meeting potential clients and business partners. Funding and business mentoring are at the heart of this network. Members looking for investment opportunities undergo a careful vetting process before becoming eligible investors. Efactor also offers a mentoring program that provides guidance to entrepreneurs through various levels in their businesses.

StartUpNation.com

In addition to offering a networking environment, Start Up Nation is packed with resourceful content including articles, blogs, podcasts and seminars, as well as forums. The content offered on this platform helps entrepreneurs to obtain suitable tools for running a successful enterprise and making informed business decisions. The topics discussed on this network are very varied to cater to the needs of entrepreneurs in a wide range of niches. Start Up Nation hosts competitions to help members develop skills in marketing, business plan creation, networking, and delivering of sales pitches.

GoBigNetwork.com

The Go Big Network helps entrepreneurs find funding. They claim that more than 300,000 startups have used them to get funding for their businesses. The network enables you to send a request for help and then links you to people within the network who can offer support or answer your question.

Spoke.com

Spoke Network is a resource for businesses and entrepreneurs looking for up-to-date information on other businesses and people. This network is especially important for sales professionals, business researchers and managers. Spoke features an information database of over 30 million companies and people in diverse industries. The network offers a platform for efficient gathering of industry specific data and news. If you are looking to understand your industry better, to keep abreast with trends, to gain access to company news and executive profiles, then this is the social network for you. As a member, you can create your own professional profile as well as one for your company. This way, other members and prospects will easily access detailed information about your company and make informed decisions that can help them partner with you.

HomeBasedBusiness.com

The Home Based Business is a free membership network of people who work from home and enjoy earning a living as self-employed business people. The network offers diverse insights into different aspects of business including opportunities, tips for running a home-based business as well as how to avoid work at home scams. Members gain access to tools that guide them through every stage of their entrepreneurial journey. As a member, you will gain access to the network's newsletter, events as well as open participation in the forum where you can ask questions, provide answers and link with other businesses in a way that is not always possible for home-based businesses.

TheFunded.com

The Funded is an online social network that enables entrepreneurs to look for funding sources, as well as review and rate these sources. As a member, you can connect with other entrepreneurs and exchange ideas on finding suitable investors. The best features of this network are that you can assess investors before doing business with them as well as receive RSS feeds of comments and announcements posted by other members. When you join the site, you will gain access to investor profiles, the investments they are involved with their investment requirements as well as their contact details.

If you are interested in learning more about online free solutions that will support your marketing and advertising campaigns, you may want to purchase The Ultimate Guide To Building And Marketing Your Online Business With Free Tools. This book will take you through some of the best tools available, will provide you with the top tips you need to succeed and will also give you a host of useful links to online resources.

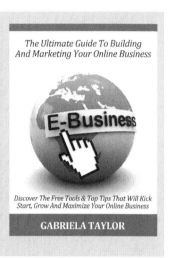

The Ultimate Guide To Building And Marketing Your Online Business

Discover The Free Tools & Top Tips That Will Kick Start, Grow And Maximize Your Online Business

GABRIELA TAYLOR

Conclusion

Throughout this book I covered some of the most popular social networks and how to use them to your advantage and grow your business. You learned how to build and engage a community across multiple social media platforms and how to become a master in creating social links.

To conclude this book, I would like to provide you with some pointers to help you manage your social networks efficiently:

Identify Where You Are

The first step in making the most of your social networks is to identify where you are and where you are not. Are you on Facebook, Twitter, Google+, StumbleUpon, LinkedIn and others that you cannot remember? Use the Checker User Names tool to help you identify which social media sites carry your username. This company also creates on your behalf, for a premium fee, up to 300 social profiles.

Select Your Platforms

A rule of thumb is to sign up to the most popular social networks including Facebook, Twitter, Google+, Pinterest, Tumblr, YouTube, StumbleUpon and LinkedIn. The reason for this is that most of your prospects and existing clients are likely to be on these platforms and you want to be where they are. Even if you are not going to use these accounts immediately, it is a good idea to secure an account on these popular sites because you will most likely use them later. Choose the platforms that will offer you and your business the greatest value and then leverage these sites.

Organize And Manage Your Social Networks

Organizing your Social Networks is very important if you are looking to take advantage of the benefits offered by all these social networks. We've seen that there are services out there such as TweetDeck or Hootsuite that enable you to schedule and post to all your social networks from a single platform, saving you time and resources.

Go Mobile

Several mobile applications make it easy for you to update your social networks on the go. This is especially helpful as a business owner who travels frequently or who simply wants to stay atop of your social media engagement.

Services like TweetDeck are accessible as a mobile application and they can help you to efficiently manage your social networks in between tasks and while you are on the move.

Stay Active

When you join so many social media sites, it is all too easy to forget others and leave them inactive. Leaving your social sites inactive can have negative impact on your social influence, is likely to drag your social media campaign and will generally give users outdated information about you. Therefore, stay actively involved in these sites. Set aside some time to offer feedback, post updates and engage with your audience.

If you enjoyed this book, I would appreciate if you could share your feedback with other Amazon readers. If you have any questions related to the topics discussed in this book, please do not hesitate to send me an email to globalndigital@gmail.com.

As I continue my research, I will make updates to this book. As you already know, I will simply do this by adding to my book and uploading the new book to Amazon. However that means that you will not get the benefit of my new research. Please send me an email to globalndigital@gmail.com so I know that you are interested in receiving updated copies of this book as soon as they are released.

Gabriela Taylor

About The Author

Gabriela Taylor is an internationally educated Global Online Marketing Strategist and Consultant who's worked with some of the world's biggest brands in Telecommunications, Retail, Lifestyle and Advertising.

A recognized expert and specialist in Social Networking, Mobile Marketing and Search Engine Optimization she is fluent in 7 languages, has lived and worked in many countries throughout the world and has experience of implementing successful web-presence strategies for both startup and large established organizations.

She is the founder of Global N' Digital, a consultancy firm specializing in Online Marketing services and Cross-Cultural business practices around the world and has also published several industry related books.

ALSO BY GABRIELA TAYLOR:

The Ultimate Guide To Marketing Your Business With...

Pinterest

A Practical Toolkit To Unlock The Web's Latest Social Networking Phenomenon

GABRIELA TAYLOR

The Ultimate Guide To Building And Marketing Your Business With ...

A Step By Step Guide To Unlocking The Power Of Google Tools And Maximizing Your Online Potential

GABRIELA TAYLOR

*The Ultimate Guide To Building
And Marketing Your Online Business*

*Discover The Free Tools & Top Tips That Will Kick
Start, Grow And Maximize Your Online Business*

GABRIELA TAYLOR

The Ultimate Guide To Marketing Your Business With…

*Using Tumblr To Leverage Social Buzz And Develop
A Brand Awareness Strategy For Your Business*

GABRIELA TAYLOR

Made in the USA
Lexington, KY
04 December 2012